Contents

FOOD GROWING WITHOUT POISONS

Meta Strandberg

TURNSTONE BOOKS

Turnstone Books
37 Upper Addison Gardens, London W14 8AJ

© 1976 Turnstone Press Ltd.

First Published in Swedish in 1974 by
Almqvist & Wiksell Förlag AB, Stockholm

ISBN 0 85500 051 1

Typesetting by Preface Ltd., Salisbury, Wilts.

Printed and bound in Great Britain by
Hazell Watson and Viney Ltd., Aylesbury, Bucks.

Preface

There has long been a need for a layman's guide with simple practical tips and rules for kitchen garden cultivation in general, but particularly for simple, organic gardening.

What then is organic gardening? There is a lot of popular misunderstanding about what it really means, derived from ignorance of the facts, from prejudice or even a kind of fear of the unknown. Yet organic gardening is not new, but is basically nature's own method of cultivation, based on a natural cycle. The balance of this cycle has been upset by man's senseless or even arrogant interference, believing that he controls nature, instead of being part of it.

While there is yet time, it is imperative that we recognise our mistaken presumptions and try to rediscover methods of growing things that will ensure Nature's co-operation, rather than waiting for her to fight back.

This doesn't mean ignoring the profit motive in agriculture. In the long term there is more profit to be gained by not exhausting the soil and not limiting the possibilities of future cultivation.

Organic and natural cultivation mean trying to improve the soil through composting, green fertilizing, rotation, mixed cropping and natural pest control.

Biodynamic cultivation has basically the same aims, but also considers the soil's relation to planetary cosmic influence. Much has been done in Sweden in recent years to combine biodynamic ideas with conventional methods in both kitchen gardening and in farming.

This book does not pretend to go into all these subtleties. It is just a simple guide. The main thing is to learn from our mistakes and our experience. The amateur gardener does not usually have time to become involved with theories. The practical gardener's first concern will be to understand the essentials — the basic needs of healthy plants.

I have therefore tried to make the opening chapters as short as possible, amplifying them with illustrations, for I have been anxious to make this guide as practical as possible. Seed choice is seldom mentioned, as this information can easily be obtained at the nearest nursery.

Meta Strandberg
Stockholm, March 1974

The Need to Cultivate

Food production is a cultural occupation. Gardening as well as farming should be considered as such by both the producers and the consumers. All cultivators are in other words cultural workers in the best tradition.

One of the purposes of organic gardening is to strengthen plant resistance to disease and pests, without unnatural agencies. The soil is a living organism and will be healthy if it is fertilised and farmed biologically. *Bios* is Greek for life; biology is the science of life, biological means according to the laws of life.

Far too often in medicine whether dealing with people, animals or plants, the emphasis is placed upon alleviating the symptoms rather than tackling the cause, or the reasons *why* a healthy person (animal, plant), becomes sick.

Isn't prevention of disease in the long term a much more productive way of safeguarding the health of coming generations? We have more chance of ensuring the health of any living organism by considering what is a reasonably healthy environment and the right nutrition for it.

Everyone must understand that, like all living things, we are subject to certain biological laws, which we disregard at our peril; the consequences may not affect us directly, but will affect our children and future generations.

Thus, it concerns life itself!

It is much more important to take some positive action than to intellectualize on the subject. Why don't we begin with the plants in our own garden? Here we have the possibility of influencing the environment creatively, a rare gift in today's world.

Even if you don't have a garden, you are not obliged to eat vegetables sprayed with insecticides. Fortunately, people are becoming aware of the dangers of chemical sprays and that naturally produced food is much healthier. This is creating a demand for foodgrowers to cultivate organically. But until many more people demand that shops stock fresh, untreated produce and nitrate-free meat, this will still be more expensive than the treated. Only when enough people insist that questionable preservatives and colouring agents be removed from food will their banning by legislation become possible.

There is a vast amount of waste land in and around most large cities. Why don't you join with other friends and organise an allotment scheme to grow vegetables and flowers? To cultivate is necessary, especially for the city dweller. How better than to grow some of your own food?

The aim of this book is to show you how easy it is to become self-sufficient in vegetables and fruit — with fresh produce that will keep you healthy.

It is easy to grow things as nature intended. If you are already a gardener, the first thing to do is to stop using artificial fertilizers. There is no need to compromise in your own garden. You must become familiar with compost heaps, natural fertilizers, waste products, hay, weeds, and other humus sources for the soil.

The reason why many of the world's most fertile areas have been reduced to sterile wastelands is because the humus, the organic material in the soil, has been exhausted. 250,000 acres in the USA alone now yield nothing and the same is true for large tracts in India, New Zealand and South Africa. This is largely a result of failure to replenish the soil regularly with organic material. Those who exploit the soil in such a way take unacceptable risks with the future. It is as irresponsible as someone who inherits a fortune and wastes it by gambling.

Healthy, alive earth = vigorous and resistant plants = vital and robust people

Soil Improvement

'I have bad soil and nothing grows in it' is a common complaint. In fact, all soils can be improved, though one type of soil is likely to be more suitable for certain kinds of plants. Each soil needs its own specific treatment. Therefore it is always advisable to have a soil analysis done at the outset. To get the best possible results you must measure the nutritional content of the soil and its *pH* value. If this is shown to be below the plant's requirements, then the nutrients in the soil cannot be exploited, even if they exist. If the *pH* level lies between 4 and 6, the soil is acidic; around 7 neutral; and over 7, alkaline.

In sand and gravel the water percolates quickly and the plant dries up easily.

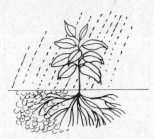

Compact soil restricts root growth and there is surface run-off as the water does not easily percolate down-wards.

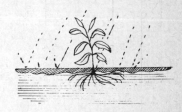

In more grainy soil, loose earth increases root growth and the plant gains more nutrition and moisture.

It is very easy and inexpensive to get a biological soil analysis done. If you are serious about growing anything, it is essential.

One is given a report on the soil's *pH* value, humus content and quality, the percentage of highly beneficial bacteria and of useful bacteria and harmful bacteria; soil structure; present cell productivity and what one can expect under cultivation, and what protective measures are needed to combat eventual soil exhaustion. Similar institutions will exist in most countries.

This is how to take a soil sample: dig vertically into the soil with a small spade and empty contents into a bucket. Repeat this several times over the ground you want analysed. Thoroughly mix the contents in the bucket and empty out ¾ of it. Mix again and empty out a further ¾ and repeat until approximately one pint volume remains. Put this into a small cloth bag, which in turn should be placed in a stiff container. Then supply your name and address and the type of cultivation you are intending.

You can, of course, attempt soil improvement using your own intuition, sound common sense and a *pH* indicator.

The following table shows different soil types, their characteristics and their potential for improvement.

Soil type	Structure	Advantages	Disadvantages	Measures for Improvement
Gravel	Stony	Lets water through easily. Can be worked early in the spring.	Dries out very easily.	Pick out larger surface stones, add humus compost, natural fertiliser, peat, mould, green plant fertiliser.
Sandy	Granular	Easy to work even when wet. Lets water through easily.	Dries out easily. Nutritional content easily washed away. Humus matter devoured.	Add plenty of all types of humus.
Heath	Rough, lumpy	Holds water better than sandy soil.	Hard to work, sometimes deficient in nutrients.	Takes time and patience to turn into good garden soil but with a lot of humus preparation it is possible.
Peaty	Dark brown or black. Bog-like.	Easily worked. Fertile.	Too acid for most plants.	Drain. Add lime mixed with sand.
Leafy	Dark grey/ black, powder structure	Ideal garden soil. Easily worked, warm and humus rich.	Often needs liming.	Loosen soil so it does not become compacted. Add lime if required.
Clay	Clumpy or lumpy. Plastic. Easy to shape.	Variable nutritious content. Withholds water and nutrition better than coarse soils. Fairly rich; good cultivating soil if correctly prepared.	Cold, hard and difficult to work when wet or dry.	Drain, Autumn digging (not deeper than 4″ (10 cm). Liming gives structure to soil. Straw-rich stable manure gives best results.

Instead of Digging

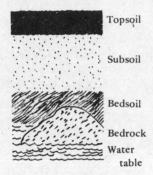

Topsoil

Subsoil

Bedsoil

Bedrock

Water table

The topsoil is the most fertile; it is the living part of the soil, rich in bacteria. Topsoil can vary in depth from 2" to 40" in mature, well-kept gardens. The subsoil is the soil strata under the topsoil and is dead and unproductive. It is light in colour as it lacks humus.

Opinions differ about the value of autumn digging in the garden. Some people insist that digging improves drainage and aerates the soil; other say worms do this as well, if not better. If you choose to dig, don't go deeper than 4"–6", otherwise you risk burying the top soil and bringing up the unusable subsoil. There is also the risk that undecayed organic matter (which may ferment), will be buried too deep. Here it will rot and become poisonous to the plant roots, instead of naturally decomposing near the surface with the help of aerobic bacteria and fungi.

All organic matter, whether fresh or partly decomposed, is completely safe when it is near the surface. It warms the soil and gives it the necessary granular structure and best nutrition.

All fertilizer and compost should therefore be raked into the surface soil and never dug in.

This rule is fundamental to natural cultivation. If the soil's working capacity is to be preserved, one should not agitate it by deep digging or turning. This does not mean that the soil is not to be prepared! Heavy clay and heathy soils require a lot of work by loosening and shallow autumn digging before one can get the living, leafy, loamy soil that is ideal for most plants. In fact, a sturdy hoe works very well in preparing the soil and loosening and mixing in the fertilizer.

Plant nutrition

Neither people nor plants can live without sun, air, water and soil. Plants obtain the right combination of these elements by a process called photosynthesis.

Plants absorb carbon dioxide from the air and with the help of sunlight and warmth, together with chlorophyll (the green colouring of plants) and water, the leaves synthesise nutrients, predominantly sugar and starch, but also fats and proteins. The atmosphere contains no more than 0.03% carbon dioxide, which is maintained by such things as the plankton of the oceans, respiratory processes of plants, animals and men, and the decay of organic matter.

The synthesised nutrients are then channelled through the stalk or outer layers of the stems, to the plant's different parts. Flowers need specially large amounts of nutrients for pollination. Even the roots get nutrients from the leaves. The nutrients absorbed by the root, like N, P, K, (sodium, phosphorous and potassium), (especially through the fine hairs, etc.) are used by the plant for growth, reserve food, etc.

Excess water evaporates (maintaining an even temperature among other things) from the leaves, through the stomata situated on the ventral surface and as drops from the hydrathodes usually found on the leaf margin and upper epidermis.

The essential nutrients for all green plants are: carbon, oxygen, hydrogen, nitrogen, potassium, calcium, phosphorous, sulphur, iron, magnesium, silicon, sodium and chlorine; these are called the major elements. Other compounds such as aluminium, manganese, boron, zinc, bromine, copper, fluorine, molybdenum, iodine and cobalt are also necessary, but in smaller amounts: these are the trace elements.

Carbon and *oxygen*, as we noted, are extracted from the air by plants — though most of the oxygen comes from the water, together with hydrogen.

Nitrogen: though 80% of the atmosphere is made up of nitrogen, only a minority of plants can use it (see p. 44). Thus, plants obtain their nitrogen requirements for protein production from the ground, in the form of nitrates and ammonium salts.

As nitrogen effects plant size and stimulates leaf growth, it is used in farming and gardening to obtain larger specimens. This forced growth means that the plant's 'skin' cannot quite keep pace; it becomes thin and fungi and insects gain hold more easily. This also results in a lot of produce being deficient in protein. Metabolism is not completed and simple nitrogen compounds, such as nitrate, remain in the food.

Nitrate can, through bacterial action, change into poisonous nitrite, which is harmful to the heart and circulation. Overdoses of nitrogen, which has also been shown to poison ground water is, with the exhaustion of the soil's humus content, the biggest threat to future life on the earth.

Potassium influences the quality of fruits and flowers and increases resistance against disease; it also helps plants' winter constitution. An excess of potassium, by causing a magnesium and calcium deficiency, will upset the plants' balance.

Calcium improves the structure of the soil, helping the plant to benefit from the various nutrients in the soil and preventing it absorbing poisonous matter (e.g. excess sulphur).

Phosphorous stimulates root growth and hastens flowering, fruit growth and ripening.

Sulphur is a necessary plant food that is usually found in sufficient quantity in the soil.

Iron and *Magnesium* are necessary for forming the chlorophyll in plants' leaves, for example.

Sodium facilitates the intake of potassium for the plant, amongst other things.

Silicon Silicon-rich plants are more resistant to fungi and pests. If the plants we eat are silicon deficient, then our skin, hair and teeth suffer as a result.

FERTILISING

There are many ways of improving your crop. One way is to stimulate the living processes within the soil, thereby encouraging the plants' own processes. Adding artificial salts in order to force growth in fact decreases the plants' own activity. By adding natural material that is lacking in the particular soil type one helps the soil's living bacteria. The nutrients that the plants need result from the natural activity of the bacteria that you have thus stimulated. It is just not possible to achieve this balanced availability of plant nutrients through the use of artificial fertilisers. Think of the analogy of human needs — you can probably see that you are not helping the natural processes of the body by relying on artificial stimulants.

Natural fertilisers should ideally be added and mixed into the soil in the autumn, to allow it to break up before the growing period begins.

Sheep manure is very rich and *horse manure* somewhat less rich in nutrition; they make the soil dry, warm and porous and break up quickly into a crumbly structure, which makes the elements accessible to the plants. *Cow manure* is more moist, more concentrated and needs more time to decompose. *Pig manure* is wet and cold and decomposes very slowly. *Hen manure* is very nitrogen rich.

Decaying hay has the same qualities as horse manure and is the best plant food that exists. It mixes well with soil, sand or clay.

Compost is sometimes not particularly nutrient rich, especially when it is made up only of plant debris, its main purpose being to stimulate life within the soil. In organic cultivation, the addition of a natural humus like compost is closest to nature's way. 'Composting' see page 16.

Peat is rich in carbon, consisting of plant matter that has been broken down without being exposed to oxygen. Mixed in the soil it increases the oxygen content and helps to retain water. However, you must remember that light brown immature peat dug into the soil will tap some of the nitrogen content in the soil, for further decomposition of the peat, and possibly short-changing the plants. Alternately, the peat that is placed on top, as surface cover, does not steal nitrogen.

Bone and *hornmeal* are good phosphorous fertilisers in ready organic form. The soil's micro-organisms have to help the plants in absorbing this beneficial and long lasting fertilizer.

Meat, blood and *fish* meals are animal waste products, organically rich in nitrogen. They are profitably used during the spring, while preparing for seeding and planting.

Limestone and *dolomite lime* both work slowly, long and evenly and therefore can be used earlier than other limes (farm lime), when liming is necessary. They can be sprinkled on the ground in the late winter or at least one month before other fertilisers and should not be applied again for at least another three months. Dolomite lime also contains magnesium.

Seaweeds are processed as a commercial fertiliser. One is called *Algomin* and is an excellent fertiliser, with most of the constituents of manure. *SPS* is a concentrate of fresh wild plants. It is effective on cuttings to promote rapid and strong root development.

Stone-meal is very beneficial, especially in large scale natural cultivation. It is rich in silicon, calcium, potassium, magnesium and many of the nutrients of manure. It can be added to soil or compost in autumn or spring. It gives better results on lighter soils, but even clay can be treated now and again.

Wood ash contains a lot of potassium, calcium, phosphorous. It is best spread in the spring when the plants have the greatest need for nutrients.

Nettle powder generally strengthens plants, partly as a soil mixture and partly as a medicine to help cure plants of fungi and pest damage. To make the solution, put nettle powder or fresh nettle leaves in a bucket and add water in the ratio 1:10. Allow this to stand for a few days — although not until it begins to smell — and either use the solution as it stands, or dilute it further by up to ten times.

Horsetail is laid fresh or prepared in water in the same way as nettles. Horsetail must, however, stand several weeks before one uses it as a liquid. The plant contains a large amount of active silicon which stimulates and increases resistance against disease. One can also buy ready prepared silicon additives, which encourage ripening and are mostly used for cabbage, strawberries, onions and tomatoes.

Green fertilisers are clover, peas or other nitrogen gathering plants, cultivated either as a middle crop or during the autumn for mixing after the first frost. Green fertiliser plants have the ability to exploit those nutrients that are normally trapped in the soil's silicon rich layers and by stone particles. When this green fertiliser later decays, the cultivated plants benefit as nitrogen is released. After they have been mixed into the soil, their roots remain as fine humus rich channels through which moisture can rise up to the topsoil.

When soil has been compacted by heavy farm machinery, the plants have great difficulty in sending their roots down in the compacted soil and cannot reach the nutrients and water. Adding green fertiliser is beneficial in these conditions.

How to make a compost heap

Composting is a process that is as old as the soil itself. Small bacteria (micro-organisms) with an enormous appetite lie dormant in the soil ready to feed on any form of organic material. When fallen leaves, branches and dead plants come into contact with the soil and its moisture, the bacteria begin to break them down. They contribute to the cycle of life by converting dead organisms into the basic nutritional elements needed by plants.

You can encourage the same nutritional cycle in your garden, for composting changes all natural refuse into fertile soil. A well-laid compost heap can turn into a healthy humus-rich substance in between one and six months, depending on conditions.

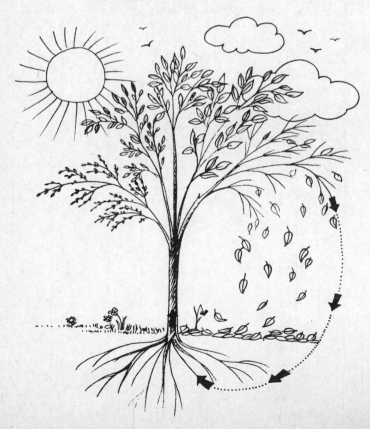

The requirements for composting are: access to refuse and enough water and air. If the compost is airtight, a certain anaerobic reaction takes place, which will make the heap rot.

Nothing happens in a dry compost. Alternatively, it must not be saturated. 50—60% moisture is about right. Adding nitrogen in the form of natural fertiliser, blood or bone meal, Algomin or similar preparations, accelerate the breakdown and make the soil richer. You can chop up refuse to make it decay quicker.

Soil is an important constituent of a compost heap, as it contains the bacteria to start the decaying process.

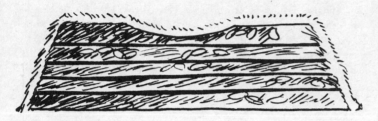

A cross section
of a compost heap.

Choose a sheltered place that is not dark or cold (e.g. not under a large tree.) Dig out a rectangle of about 6' x 4' and 6" deep. The compost must have contact with the soil.

Put down layers of course plant material at the bottom (hay, dry grass, etc.). This is good for drainage and air circulation.

Alternate the refuse (the finer the better) with layers of fertilizer (or stone meal) and soil. First spread out a layer of refuse and cover with a layer of fertilizer and/or bloodmeal, Algomin, etc. On this lay a thin layer of soil and then more plant refuse. Material that is damp and heavy should be mixed with loose, dry plant matter, i.e. hay, etc. Very loose matter should be compressed and watered.

When your refuse has run out or the heap is about 3' high, it should be sealed with a layer of soil. This soil layer (about 2" thick) contributes micro-organisms and also prevents the uppermost refuse from drying out or blowing away.

The whole compost heap should then, if possible, be covered with a warming layer (e.g. hay). Check periodically that parts of the heap are not drying out. If so, water it. Low compost heaps are preferable; air circulation is better and one does not have to turn the heap (which would otherwise have to be done once a month), to aerate and ensure even decay.

All organic material can be used in a compost heap — hay, weeds, cut grass, vegetable matter, rotten fruit, kitchen refuse that will not attract foxes or rats, coffee grains, sour milk, egg shells, berries, seaweed, reeds, sawdust, wood chippings, wood ash, and all sorts of natural fertiliser. Large amounts of leaves should be composted separately, as they take longer to decay.

One can add certain compost preparations to help bacteria to thrive. 'Symbioflor', a fermented humus additive is one example that is used in natural cultivation. (See p. 96 for ideas on biodynamics).

A compost heap can be kept neat by using a frame of chicken netting on boards, with a side that is left open, or can be opened.

Mature compost is the best growing base for seeds and nursery plants; therefore put some compost in the row when sowing. If you lay the half-decayed compost between the rows and around the plants, it restricts weeds and retains the moisture. It is also the best winter covering for your beds. At the same time, it supplies constant nutrition for both soil and worms.

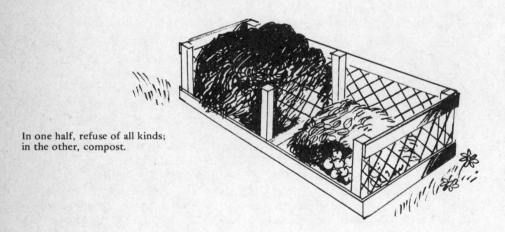

In one half, refuse of all kinds; in the other, compost.

Autumn work in the garden

The soil should be loosened up with a strong hoe or fork to a depth of approximately 4″.

If possible, sow green fertiliser of clover (Alexander or peach clover) or mustard seed. After the first frost, mix it in.

Some kind of natural fertiliser should be spread in a thin layer with some compost, which need not be fully decomposed. This gives a loose and airy covering, so that the soil and the living things within it, can breath. The soil should never be really left 'naked', without a protective cover of vegetation or decomposed compost.

In the spring the soil will be finely grained, easy to prepare, alive and rich with worms, our most co-operative allies. To emphasise the value and contribution of the worm would require a separate chapter. This is not possible, but did you know:

that a worm can in one day produce its own weight in fertilizer: about one gramme.

that worms increase the number of microbes that must be present in healthy soil. Harmful microbes are thereby kept down.

Necessary garden tools

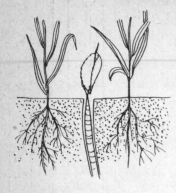

that worms break up food by eating 'small stones' which are later returned as truly rich fertiliser.

that the worm's excrement contains five times as much plant nutrition, weight for weight, as is found in the surrounding soil.

that tunnels dug by worms enable water and air to circulate in the top and subsoils.

that the worm mixes the organic and inorganic boundaries of the soil, contributing greatly to the resultant changes that take place.

that the worm eats soil and organic material and deposits fertile humus enriched with lime from the worm's lime glands.

that much harm is done to worms by lime nitrates and other artificial fertilisers.

that, although in healthy soil one can find 500 worms per square yard, on rationally treated farm land only 10 worms. Tractor ploughing and machine hoeing effectively amount to the mass murder of worms.

Improve the worm's environment!

First year	Second year	Third year

Even in small gardens, the most must be made of crop rotation — an integral part of natural cultivation. The diagram shows an example of how one sows beans which provide nitrogen, before the nutrient thirsty cauliflower. Carrots should not have too much nitrogen and therefore can be cultivated after the cauliflower.

Nursery cultivation

Plants grown indoors ready for transplanting outside. Four leaves have developed above the two primaries.

To prolong the growing season one needs, if not a greenhouse, at least some frames. Here one can begin work in late winter or early spring when the longing to start becomes uncontrollable, although the garden remains wet and unworkable. There are also peat pots and mini-frames for those who have room indoors — here you can start pottering about in January.

In the South one can start using a warm frame in February/March and in Scotland in March/April. With a semi-warm frame we should begin a month later with a cold frame one should wait a further 14 days, depending on the weather conditions.

Use a thin spatula or a knife for the more delicate plants.

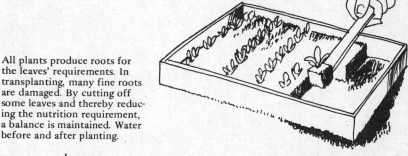

All plants produce roots for the leaves' requirements. In transplanting, many fine roots are damaged. By cutting off some leaves and thereby reducing the nutrition requirement, a balance is maintained. Water before and after planting.

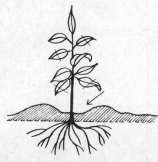

Put a little extra soil around the plant and hollow out to capture the rainwater.

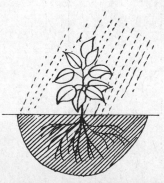

Plenty of watering soaks down into the soil and encourages deep root growth to where there is catchment matter.

Too little "sprinkling" makes the roots spread out near the surface, making plants vulnerable to hoeing, sun and wind.

You can make your own frame, using treated wooden boards and covering with old window frames or plastic.

Place the frame in a sheltered, warm corner of the garden, preferably facing south to maximise heat and light. Put a rug on top as a protection against frost or a strong sun. Remember to air during warm days.

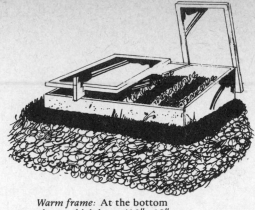

Semi-warm frame
Use about 10″ (25 cm) of horse manure, covered by about 8″ (20 cm) of soil.

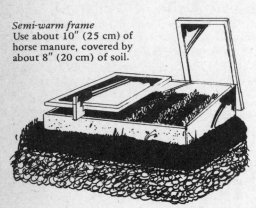

Warm frame: At the bottom place a thick layer (12″–18″, 30–40 cm) of organic material, preferably horse manure. Cover this with a 6″ (15 cm) layer of garden soil or compost. The manure will "burn" under this soil layer and give out warmth and carbon dioxide.

Mini-tropical greenhouse
6′8″ x 4″ x 3′2″ high
200 x 120 x 95 cm

Cold frame
This is placed directly on the ground.

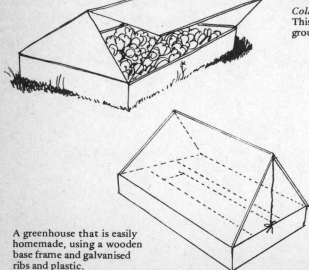

A greenhouse that is easily homemade, using a wooden base frame and galvanised ribs and plastic.

These miniature greenhouses are merely wire arches covered with plastic.

22

Plant protection

When you consider all the various pesticides that have been spread out over our fields and gardens in the last decade, you would think that all the pests must have been wiped out. Instead, they are more numerous and even plant diseases are on the increase (degeneration?)

Many people have been affected, sometimes fatally, by pesticides. The effect on bird life could already be seen in the 1960's from Rachel Carson's book *Silent Spring*.

Useful insects are exterminated with the pests, but the former seem less able to regenerate themselves. Entire bee colonies have been wiped out by spraying flowers.

How do these poisons affect people?

1—2 grammes of DDT damages the autonomic nervous system. Long term effects can lead to chronic brain damage (in Sweden, but not in all countries, DDT. is forbidden).

Carbolic agents used on fruit can cause serious burns.

Hexa preparation is poisonous to liver, kidneys and nerves.

Mercury mixtures are extremely poisonous and damage the liver, kidneys and nervous system.

Dieldrin-Aldrin, used against the carrot fly, has been found to be active in carrot juice six months after application.

Copper and sulphur pesticide sprays are used up to ten times a season on fruit crops.

The list could continue — there are over 100 varieties of poisonous pesticides. Attack by disease or pests means that there is something wrong with our ideas of cultivation. We must think again of building up the health of the soil and plants. If we make sure that the soil has enough fertile humus, pests usually do not become a problem.

Ground cover, good compost and other fertilisers and loosening without digging or turning can make soil healthy again within a few years.

You must also make sure to choose the places where the plants will do well and also not to cultivate the same plants in the same place, year after year. You should make full use of crop rotation, even in a small garden.

GROWING TOGETHER

Some plants flourish together, others do not. One explanation can be that plants with deep roots loosen up compact soil to allow plants with smaller roots to increase their nutritional catchment areas.

The table below shows which plants stimulate and protect each other and which should not be planted next to each other.

Vegetables	Likes	Dislikes
beans	potatoes, cucumber, cauliflower, cabbage and herbs	onions, garlic, beetroot
fennel		tomatoes
chives	carrots	peas, beans
cucumber	beans, corn, peas, Jerusalem artichokes	potatoes, herbs, tomatoes, radishes, black radishes
strawberries	beans, spinach, onions	cabbage
Jerusalem artichokes	cucumbers	potatoes
swede	peas, onions	
cabbage family (except red cabbage)	all herbs and aromatic varieties	tomatoes
onions	carrots, strawberries, lettuce, tomatoes, radishes	beans, peas
corn	potatoes, peas, beans, squash, cucumber	tomatoes
carrots	onions, peas, herbs, tomatoes, radishes	dill
parsley	asparagus, tomatoes	
potatoes	beans, maize	cucumber, squash, Jerusalem artichokes, tomatoes, peas . raspberries
leeks	carrots, onions, celery	beans, peas
radishes	peas, lettuce, carrots, onions	cucumber
beetroots	onions, turnip cabbage, cabbage	beans
lettuce	carrots, radishes, strawberries, cucumber	
celery	onions, tomatoes, cabbage	
soya beans	grow well everywhere and with everything	
asparagus	tomatoes, parsley, basil	
spinach	strawberries	
squash	maize	
tomatoes	onions, parsley, asparagus, cabbage carrots	corn, potatoes, fennel, cucumber
peas	carrots, swedes, radishes, cucumber, corn, beans	onions, potatoes

RECOGNISE FRIENDS . . .

We must be careful of animals that can help us to protect our plants. So we must distinguish between friends and enemies.

The worm: its praises have already been sung! see page 19.

The ladybird: a single ladybird can devour 70—100 greenfly daily and the larva is hardly less voracious. It lives, otherwise, on mites and leaf flies.

The green lace-wing: the full-grown lacewing is not so bothered with greenfly. This sheer green shimmering insect with yellow eyes lives mostly on plant juice and nectar and often hibernates indoors, around windows near flower pots. But the larva live up to their name: greenfly lion. Each larva eats 200—400 greenfly before the pupa stage.

The sawfly: a very common winged parasite that lives on pollen. The larva on the contrary, which resembles a small leech (1 cm) in form and movement, can consume a greenfly a minute.

Grasshopper: always found in low vegetation. It is $1''-1\frac{1}{2}''$ (25 x 40 mm) in length and green with long wings. Greenfly, beetles and larva constitute its diet. Eggs are laid in the ground and remain there throughout the winter.

Parasitic insects: these insects, found in thousands of varieties, are very important in the natural control of pests and should be encouraged on a large scale. Females have long egg laying tubes that they insert, for example, into a louse or a larva. The eggs become larvae and feed on their host, living there until they are fully developed flies.
The cabbage white's hymenoptera is the most important parasite of the cabbage white's larva.

The robberfly: the large robberfly (up to $1''$, 25 mm long), is black with a yellow haired lower back. It catches and eats even quite large insects. The larva is born in the soil and lives on other insect larvae.

The ground beetle: out of the thousands of beetles, the ground beetle does the most good in the garden. Dark brown or black, it hides in the soil during the day and in the evening starts hunting larvae, worms and slugs. Their predatory larvae make pathways on the ground and await their prey in the open. Unfortunately, worms make up a part of this greedy hunter's diet.

Bumble bees and bees: their priceless contribution is the pollination they inadvertently cause.

Common soldier beetle: the upper back is red with a black spot, the legs are black. It is, like its larva, a predator, and is often seen on unbellated flowers. The larvae are called 'snow worms' as they are often seen in late winter.

Shieldbug: Several varieties of shieldbug are predators with a specially equipped mouth which sucks nutrition from other shieldbugs or leaf pupae, butterfly larvae or greenflies. Light brown, ¾" (20 mm) long.

Spiders: all spiders are predators. The danger is that both friends and foes get caught in their webs.

The ant lion: the ant lion larva carefully digs an enclosed pit where it waits for its prey, such as ants, to fall in.

The slow-worm: often to be found in the compost heap, it lives on flies and other insects.

The frog: all frogs are helpful animals that eat flies, midges and larvae.

The toad: if one has the good fortune to have a toad in the garden, one should try hard to keep him. He eats enormous amounts of small creeping insects and slugs. Unfortunately, he is becoming less common, but once arrived he usually stays — the toad is a confirmed creature of habit.

The bat: at dusk, the bat begins his hunt for all sorts of insects, moths and cockchafers.

The mole: each day, the mole eats more than its own weight in food. Unfortunately this includes worms and cock chafer's larvae and other larvae and small mice.

The mouse: the mouse is a greedy insect hunter.

The hedgehog: this rarer and rarer animal lives on mice, larvae, slugs and insects.

Thrushes, bullfinches, starlings, wagtails, swallows and tits: make sure that birds inhabit your garden. They will bring great benefit.

. . . AND ENEMIES

Greenfly: found in groups on the undersides of leaves, or on young shoots. They suck juice from the plant. Ladybirds and stinkbug larvae will control them. You can help by hosing them away with a strong jet of water. The greenfly comes when plant circulation is disturbed and contains too much sugar. Nettle water can restore the balance. (see page 14).

Black fly: found usually on broad beans. For large attacks apply warm water, nettlewater or bracken extract. Cultivate broad beans together with potatoes. Try to encourage early flowering.

Fleas: the striped flea-beetle is 1/10th inch long and especially likes cabbage and radishes. If the plant is agitated, on can see them jumping. They prefer warm and dry weather, Powder rows and plants with Algomin or wood ash. Normal flour or simply fine soil that is sprinkled on the plant keeps this pest away.

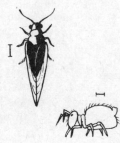

Carrot flea: sucks on young plant leaves, causes gooseberry blight. The leaf becomes deformed and dies. The plant growth is checked or it dies.

Lucerne flea: a jumper often mistaken for other fleas. Likes to attack beans and peas. Chews leaf buds and makes holes in leaves.

The carrot and onion flies: the carrot fly lays eggs next to delicate young carrots. The 5 mm long, yellowish-white larvae eat the roots so that the small plants die. The closely related onion fly larva attacks onions, turning their leaves yellow and rotting the plants.

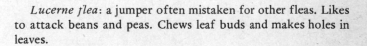

Do not sow on soil that has been newly treated with fresh fertiliser. These flies do not occur on healthy, composted soil. Plant carrots and onions together. If you do get an attack, dowse the plants with a strong-smelling tea of some pungent plant, i.e. mint or wormwood, etc.

The carrot fly can also sometimes attack celeriac. Blue spots are then formed on the roots. Fresh humus will help to build up the plant's own resistance.

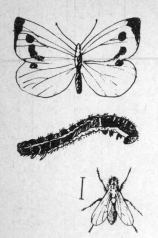

The cabbage white: the 1½—2″ (40—50 mm) long larvae can quickly devour all sorts of cabbage leaves. 2 or 3 generations mature in a season.

The simplest method is to hand pick them away. Cultivate tomatoes or some strong smelling herbs together with the cabbage. Don't leave damaged leaves in the patch. The strong smell of rotten cabbage can attract these pests.

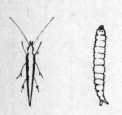

The large and small root cabbage fly: these flies lay their eggs next to young cabbage plants and the larvae eat their way into the roots and kill the plants. After planting, sprinkle woodash on and around the cabbage plants. The cabbage root fly will not lay its eggs in the loose ash.

The cabbage caterpillar: another yellowish-green butterfly larva that is about 1 cm long and that is difficult to detect once it has eaten its way into the cabbage leaves. It also attacks swedes and turnips. Control cabbage cultivation with even spacing and break up the eggs on the underside of the leaves.

Cabbage fly: lives on cross flowering plants such as cabbages, radishes, mustard etc. Like other flies, has many enemies.

Cabbage gall weevil: causes roots to swell up, which can be mistaken for club root, another cabbage disease. In the case of the weevil, it is their small white larvae that do the damage. Burn old and infected roots.

The pea moth: small with broad wings. It lays its eggs on the leaves of the flowering pea plant. The yellowish-white maggots develop with the help of a protective thread-like cocoon around the leaf. They eat the peas in the pods. Burn infected plants.

The thrips: this 1 mm long insect, sucks on leaves and pods so that they become distorted and turn grey. Pick out and burn infected plants.

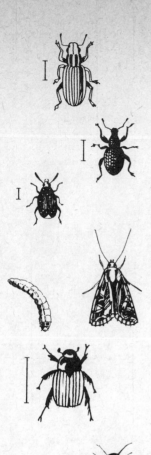

Pea weevil: causes considerable damage to wild and culti-vated pod plants, especially in dry, warm weather. The typical notched leaves show that the weevil has been feeding. The larvae live off and in the root nodules.
Burn diseased plants.

Ear weevil: the larvae live in the roots of different plants and sometimes damage strawberries and rasberries and decor-ative plants.

Bean weevil: there are about ten varieties, but they are rather rare in smaller gardens. The larvae develop in pod plants.

Flies: there are many kinds of flies, whose larvae can be destructive. They feed at ground level off the young plants of potatoes, onions, cabbages, and damage fruit trees and bushes. Handpicking them from the highest soil patch in the vicinity is recommended.

Garden cock chafer: metallic green or blue beetle with reddish brown wing markings, which gnaws at leaves and flowers. The larvae gnaw the roots and can cause considerable damage to potatoes, fruit and berries, etc.

Wireworm (Leather jackets): the brown, jointed, tough larva becomes an oblong, flat, usually black beetle. This leaps with a clicking sound and rights itself if it has landed on its back. Leather jackets prefer newly dug soil that formerly grew grass, or dry, hard soil. They eat roots, often of potatoes, lettuces, carrots and cabbages.
Do not cultivate root vegetables on ground that has formerly supported grass. Keep the soil loose and rich in humus. Put out some loose potatoes here and there and check them daily. Lime (although not on the potato patch!). Use an onion solution as a deterrent (onion or leaf of onion in water overnight).
Moles, mice, crows, starlings, toads and beetles eat the larvae.

Woodlice: grey or brown armourplated insects that confine themselves to dark, damp places. They are destructive in frames and greenhouses only if they are allowed to multiply. Can be picked away by hand. Their hiding places should be cleaned out.

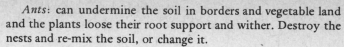

Ants: can undermine the soil in borders and vegetable land and the plants loose their root support and wither. Destroy the nests and re-mix the soil, or change it.

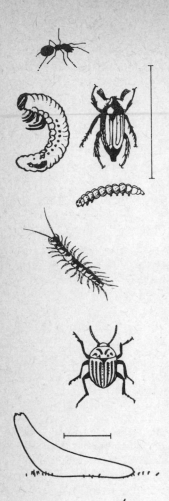

Chafer grubs: fat, curved, yellowy-white larvae that gnaw holes in potatoes and other root crops. Can be picked away by hand.

Cut worms: cut worm larvae can sometimes cause considerable damage to plant roots in the garden.

Centipedes: the 1″−1½″ (25−40 mm) long, brown, shiny centipede rolls into a ball when disturbed (a white variety that looks like a worm doesn't do this). Centipedes can gnaw holes in newly sewn beans and peas and occasionally in potatoes, though they don't usually cause widespread damage. By nursing peas and beans and then transplanting, such attacks are prevented.

The colorado beetle: both the larva and the beetle voraciously eat the foliage of potato plants and large crops can be completely ruined. The beetle can be picked away by hand on smaller cultivations and it is one's duty to let the authorities know of an attack by this pest.

Slugs: juicy leaves growing close to the ground are sometimes liable to a slug invasion, especially during damp conditions. Sprinkle wood ash on lime and pick them away by hand.

Gooseberry saw fly: the larva has only two pairs of belly feet and moves forward by arching its body. Its favourite food is gooseberry leaves, but it can also attack blackthorn and bird-cherry.

Tortoiseshell larva: the butterfly's larva lives on the leaves of blackcurrants and nettles and other varieties.

SAFE SPRAYS

Naturally, we hope our friends will take care of our enemies in the garden. However, problems can occur, even though the building up of natural resistance through biological control (mixed cropping, rotation and hand picking), have all helped. There are some safe sprays made from plant extract that can be used in emergencies. These are broken down completely naturally and are not dangerous to humans or to household animals, but are deadly to insects and larvae.

Pyrethrine: an extract from chrysanthemums that is a well-known insect repellent.

Derris: the crushed roots of the derris plant contains rotenone which paralyses or kills many cold-blooded animals, e.g. insects and fish. Rotenone repels and kills most sucking and gnawing insects. Its effect lasts for some time.

Quassia: Quassia comes from the wood of a tropical tree. A boiled solution contains agents that kill certain insects but are not harmful to humans or other animals. The spray works on direct contact and is best against thin skinned pests.

Another safe spray is 54°C warm water. Even the most sensitive plant can stand this temperature, but plant insects without 'skin' and naked larvae succumb at 45°C. Beetles die at 50°C. All plants, branches and roots that will bend can be dipped and protected in this way. This warm water method I find ideal for berry bushes and small fruit trees.

DISEASES

Plants can wither and die without insect attacks. They can, despite help, be overtaken by bacteria, virus or fungi.

The illustrations facing p. 25 show diseases that can also threaten your garden.

I have already mentioned nettle water as a vitamin injection for languishing plants. There are several mixtures that can strengthen resistance and act as a medicine. Extracts from various plant types such as horsetail, onions, horse radishes, wood worm, for example, work well against fungi diseases.

Horsetail, like stinging nettles, contains a lot of silicon. Repeated spraying or watering increases the silicon content of the leaves, which strengthens them and makes it more difficult for the fungi and bacteria to force themselves into the cell tissue.

Boil up 50 grams of horsetail in about 4 pints of water for at least half an hour. Strain and dilute with water until you have approximately 2½ gallons of solution. To be used against mildew, scab, mould and other fungus diseases.

At the risk of nagging, I want to reiterate the importance of preventive measures. When a healthy balance in the garden has been obtained, then these pages on pests and diseases are no longer relevant.

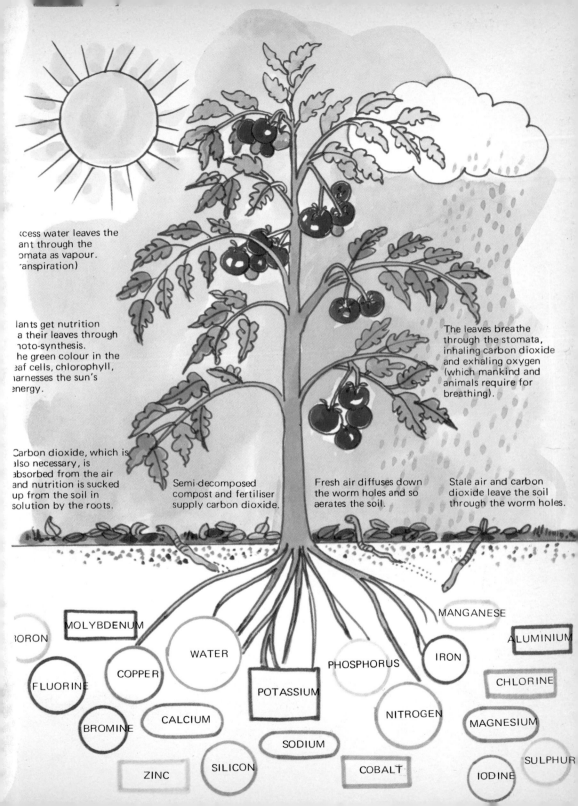

Excess water leaves the plant through the stomata as vapour. (Transpiration)

Plants get nutrition via their leaves through photo-synthesis. The green colour in the leaf cells, chlorophyll, harnesses the sun's energy.

The leaves breathe through the stomata, inhaling carbon dioxide and exhaling oxygen (which mankind and animals require for breathing).

Carbon dioxide, which is also necessary, is absorbed from the air and nutrition is sucked up from the soil in solution by the roots.

Semi-decomposed compost and fertiliser supply carbon dioxide.

Fresh air diffuses down the worm holes and so aerates the soil.

Stale air and carbon dioxide leave the soil through the worm holes.

MANGANESE

MOLYBDENUM

BORON

ALUMINIUM

WATER

COPPER

IRON

PHOSPHORUS

FLUORINE

CHLORINE

POTASSIUM

CALCIUM

NITROGEN

MAGNESIUM

BROMINE

SODIUM

ZINC

SILICON

COBALT

SULPHUR

IODINE

Our friends

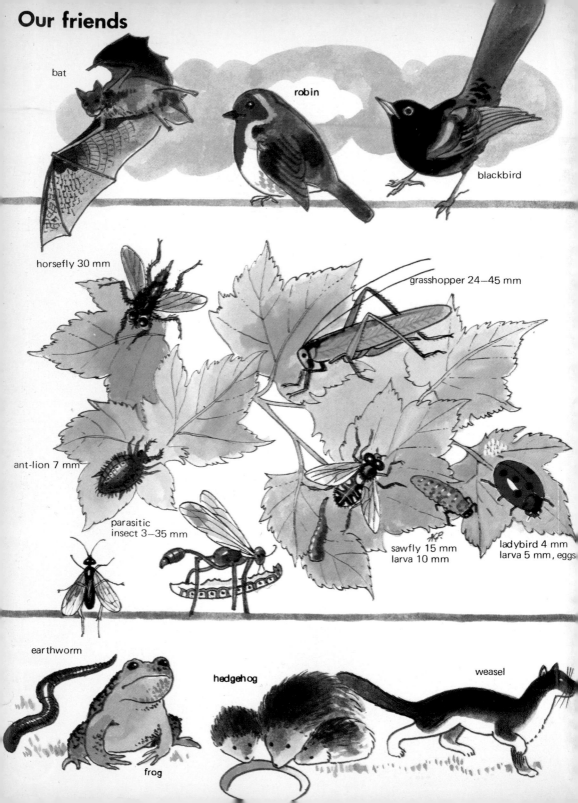

bat

robin

blackbird

horsefly 30 mm

grasshopper 24—45 mm

ant-lion 7 mm

parasitic
insect 3—35 mm

sawfly 15 mm
larva 10 mm

ladybird 4 mm
larva 5 mm, eggs

earthworm

hedgehog

weasel

frog

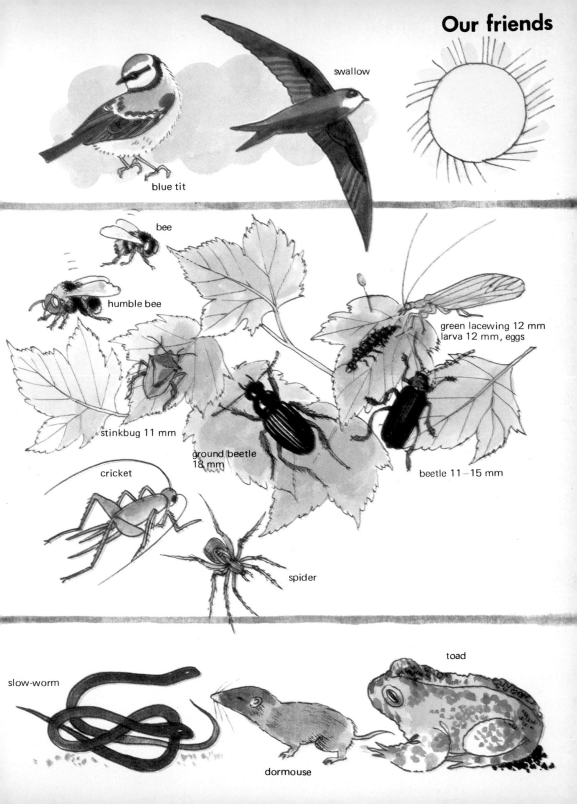

Our friends

swallow

blue tit

bee

humble bee

green lacewing 12 mm
larva 12 mm, eggs

stinkbug 11 mm

ground beetle
18 mm

beetle 11–15 mm

cricket

spider

slow-worm

dormouse

toad

Some diseases in the kitchen garden

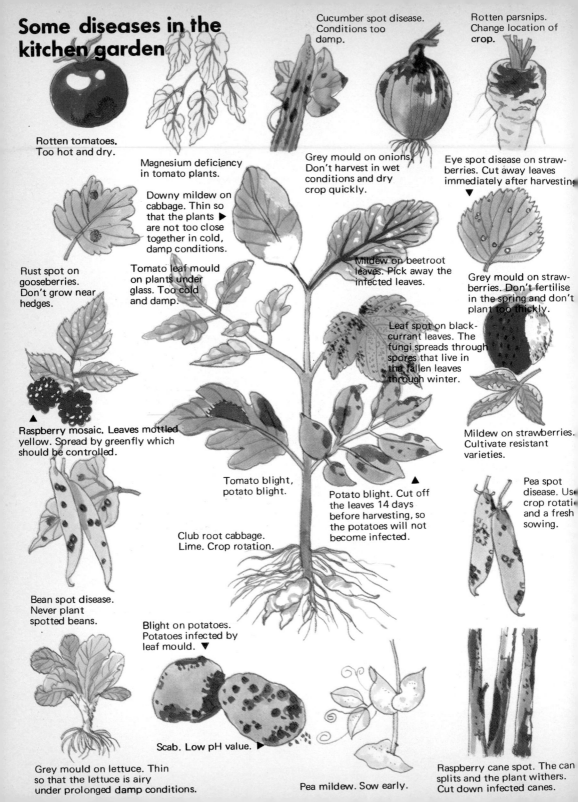

Rotten tomatoes. Too hot and dry.

Cucumber spot disease. Conditions too damp.

Rotten parsnips. Change location of crop.

Magnesium deficiency in tomato plants.

Grey mould on onions. Don't harvest in wet conditions and dry crop quickly.

Eye spot disease on strawberries. Cut away leaves immediately after harvesting

Downy mildew on cabbage. Thin so that the plants ▶ are not too close together in cold, damp conditions.

Rust spot on gooseberries. Don't grow near hedges.

Tomato leaf mould on plants under glass. Too cold and damp.

Mildew on beetroot leaves. Pick away the infected leaves.

Grey mould on strawberries. Don't fertilise in the spring and don't plant too thickly.

Leaf spot on blackcurrant leaves. The fungi spreads through spores that live in the fallen leaves through winter.

▲ Raspberry mosaic. Leaves mottled yellow. Spread by greenfly which should be controlled.

Mildew on strawberries. Cultivate resistant varieties.

Tomato blight, potato blight.

Potato blight. Cut off the leaves 14 days before harvesting, so the potatoes will not become infected.

Pea spot disease. Use crop rotation and a fresh sowing.

Club root cabbage. Lime. Crop rotation.

Bean spot disease. Never plant spotted beans.

Blight on potatoes. Potatoes infected by leaf mould. ▼

Scab. Low pH value. ▶

Pea mildew. Sow early.

Grey mould on lettuce. Thin so that the lettuce is airy under prolonged damp conditions.

Raspberry cane spot. The cane splits and the plant withers. Cut down infected canes.

Easily cultivated vegetables

LEAF VEGETABLES

Lettuce

100 g lettuce gives:
13 calories
95 g water
1.0 g protein
0.1 g fat
1.7 g carbohydrate
18 mg calcium
21 mg phosphorous
0.5 mg iron
33 units vitamin A
0.04 mg thiamine
0.05 mg riboflavin
0.01 mg niacin
13 mg vitamin C

Of all the home grown vegetables, the leafy ones are those which differ most in taste and quality from the commercially grown (especially if imported). Lettuce is an easily grown vegetable that gives a rich harvest and should have a place even in the smallest garden. Since it is frost-resistant it can be sown as soon as the soil is workable. Thinning can begin when the leaves are about 2″ (5 cm) long, i.e. ready for eating. In this way you can eat lettuce from early spring, even without frames. If sowing is staggered, you can have fresh lettuce well into the autumn, especially when using the loose leaf and iceberg varieties. The most common types are:

Cabbage lettuce: early. Row spacing 14″–16″ (35–40 cm). Plant spacing 8″ (20 cm) after thinning. Begin harvesting after 5–6 weeks.

Cos lettuce: the earliest and easiest to grow. Row spacing 8″–12″ (20–30 cm). Harvested earlier than cabbage lettuce and goes to seed later. Can be harvested after 4–5 weeks.

Iceberg: sown somewhat later. Develops slowly. Second sowing should take place about one month after the first. This lettuce is more particular about its soil and fertilizer. Keeps well in storage. Row spacing 15″–16″ (40–50 cm). Space between plants 12″ (30 cm). Can start harvesting after 6–8 weeks.

Soil conditions

Lettuce is not particular and will grow on most soils, though the ideal is of leafy quality, loose and limey (*pH* value 7.0–7.5).

Plant care

Lettuce grown in healthy soil should be pest free. Possibly during a wet autumn small slugs may occur, but these can easily be picked away by hand. Alternatively, sprinkle ashes or lime to disperse them.

Nettles

Nettles are one of our most health-giving and nutrition-rich plants. They have potassium, calcium, iron, phosphorous, silicon

and sulphur and they contain considerable amounts of Vitamins A and C.

Traditionally, all country gardens had a nettle patch and if your garden is not too small, it would be healthy to maintain this tradition. Throughout the summer one can pick the small shoots and use them for soups and stews, or dry them for winter needs. Dried, they can be crumbled easily and sprinkled into many dishes, or used as an ingredient for bread, for example. I always have a dried bunch of nettles hanging in the kitchen near the stove. A little iron here and there may prevent thin blood in the spring!

In chemists and health shops one can buy a preparation of dried nettles as a tonic to build-up and clean the blood.

Nettles are not only healthy for people, they also make a simple preparation to stimulate plant growth, improve the soil and strengthen resistance to pests (see p. 14).

So sow them in the stoniest corner of your garden!

Dandelions

You probably don't want to know about them and perhaps they already grow in your garden whether you like it or not! However, in France and Germany the dandelion is actually cultivated, at least in the winter, for its vitamin C rich leaves in salads — and delicious wine can be made from the flowers. Even the roots are nutritious — containing protein and inulin and (with preparation), are a worthy addition to several dishes.

Spinach

100 g spinach gives:
21 calories
93 g water
2.3 g protein
0.3 g fat
2.1 g carbohydrate
22 mg calcium
50 mg phosphorous
3 mg iron
840 units of vitamin A
0.08 mg thiamine
0.24 mg riboflavin
0.9 mg niacin
0.9 mg vitamin C

Spinach can be sown in either autumn or spring. It is one of the most frost-resistant kitchen plants. It is also a plant that should be home grown. High nitrate concentrations (harmful to both animals and people), have been found in commercially grown spinach and the outer leaves of cabbage and iceberg lettuce. Spinach has a high content of oxalates. People prone to kidney stones should avoid it.

There can be several sowings in the spring and towards autumn. During a warm, dry summer it often flowers. It is good to have spinach as the first spring crop.

Row spacing 10" (25 cm). Space between mature plants for thinning 5"—6" (10—15 cm).

Soil conditions
Spinach is fussy, needing an extremely rich, leafy, damp soil (*pH* value 7), without which it runs to seed.

Spinach Beet

Instead of spinach, you can cultivate spinach beet as an alternative crop with a large harvest. Spinach beet belongs to the beet family and does not contain oxalic acid. It is perhaps practical to cultivate spinach early in the spring, while throughout the summer and towards winter (in a mild autumn), cut leaves off the spinach beet plants, which soon regenerate. The leaves can be eaten like spinach and the 1½″ stalks can be boiled and served with butter and are as tasty as the most delicate asparagus.

The spinach beet is frost-resistant and continues to produce new leaves until the ground begins to freeze. Next spring it sprouts again if the winter has not been too severe. (At the time of writing both the spinach beet and the iceberg lettuce are growing in my garden despite several frosts, even up to −10°C.)

Row spacing: 16″ (40 cm). Plant spacing after thinning: 10″ (25 cm).

Soil conditions

Spinach beet is easily cultivated, but prefers leafy, damp, alkaline soil (*pH* value 7.5).

Plant care

Spinach and spinach beet, as far as I know, do not have any enemies, save sometimes the field fly larvae which are almost invisible on the leaf, but on boiling turn white. Woodash on and around the small plants hinders the fly's activity.

Dill

Dill really belongs to the herb garden, but even without one there should be a place reserved for this originally oriental multi-purpose herb.

Dill can be sown from April and at intervals throughout the summer so that there is always a fresh supply and enough for deep freezing or drying for the winter.

Row spacing: 12″−16″ (30−40 cm).

Soil conditions

Rich, leafy soil (*pH* value 7).

Plant care

During warm summers and conditions unfavourable to the plant, dill can be attacked by *greenfly*. Water with a nettle solution (see p. 14). Sow parsley in alternate rows, as its smell acts as a repellant to the greenfly.

Parsley

100 g parsley gives:
43 calories
79 g water
5 g protein
0. 2 g fat
5 g carbohydrate
325 mg calcium
130 mg phosphorous
8 mg iron
1000 units of vitamin A
0. 08 mg thiamine
0. 30 mg riboflavin
120 mg vitamin C

Parsley is another herb that no garden should be without. Parsley grows very slowly and must be sown early. It can be practical to seed rows with some radishes, as these grow quickly and soon make the rows visible for weeding and hoeing. Once the parsley has taken, it grows without any problems.

Row spacing: 14″ (35 cm).

I keep parsley which is rich in iron and vitamins A and C in dry bunches by my stove, and as a finely chopped preparation in my refrigerator. (Don't forget to put out a little parsley in the kitchen cupboards of your summer cottages. It keeps away the creepy-crawlies!)

The curley-leafed variety is usually grown, though the smooth leafed variety has a stronger aroma. This may be because the former cannot be mistaken for the poisonous wild parsley, or perhaps it is just prettier? The wild parsley's leaves glisten as though they have been varnished. They also have an unpleasant smell, resembling garlic.

Soil conditions

Biennial parsley flourishes in fertile loamy soil. You should sow it early, while there is still moisture in the soil.

Plant care

No pests will trouble parsley!

CABBAGE

Cabbages have many enemies and considering how the war against these is waged in commercial cultivation, I prefer to grow my own. DDT, aldrin, arsenic, nicotine — apparently no poison is considered too strong for the cabbage fly, larva or flea. And when one further considers that cabbage fields are often bordered by roads where all types of motor pollution are absorbed by the plants' leaves . . .

When excessive nitrogen containing fertilizer is used, the plant cannot fully assimilate it and the excess remains as a nitrate. This occurs particularly with large leafed plants, such as cabbage.

Surely, therefore, one must try to cultivate at least some sorts of cabbage, even if they are not the most easily grown vegetables.

Broccoli

100 g broccoli gives:
40 calories
90 g water
3.9 g protein
0.2 g fat
5.4 g carbohydrate
37 mg calcium
78 mg phosphorous
1.0 mg iron
325 unit of vitamin A
0.05 mg thiamine
0.12 mg riboflavin
0.5 mg niacin
96 mg vitamin C

Broccoli is easier to cultivate than cauliflower or white cabbage. It is the blue-green crown and some of the stalk that is eaten. Broccoli survives hard frosts and if one staggers sowing, harvests can be obtained even in winter. Sow in a frame or in pots, and transplant in well-prepared soil when you think the coldest nights have passed. Preferably, choose a rainy day for transplanting, when the ground is sodden through.

Row spacing: 2′(60 cm). Plant spacing: 16″(40 cm). For later cultivation the seeds can be sown directly into the allocated plot.

Loosen the soil frequently and never let it dry out.

One should harvest before the buds begin to reveal their yellow flowers. After the first crown, others develop as offshoots. One should cut off the crowns with about 4″ (10 cm) of the stalk and with some small leaves — everything can be eaten.

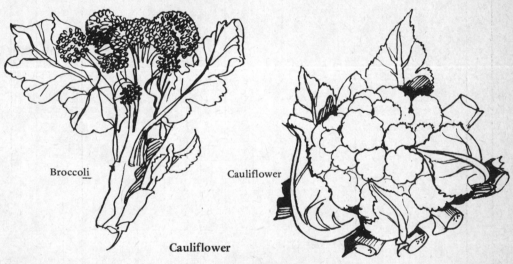

Broccoli

Cauliflower

Cauliflower

100 g cauliflower gives:
25 calories
91 g water
2.4 g protein
0.2 g fat
3.3 g carbohydrate
22 mg calcium
50 mg phosphorous
0.5 mg iron
5 units of vitamin A
0.09 mg thiamine
0.12 mg riboflavin
0.6 mg niacin
70 mg vitamin C

Cauliflower is an historical vegetable which has been cultivated here for centuries. It was known in Greece even before Christ.

If you want uninterrupted supplies from July to October, you should plant twice respectively in the spring and early summer. The cauliflower is more vulnerable to cold and frost than other cabbages. When the heads have grown so that one glimpses the white crowns, the surrounding leaves should be broken and bent over the heads. This preserves them. Harvest before the heads begin to stretch and split. Pull up the whole plant; cut off the whole crown with some small leaves and put the rest on the compost — naturally!

Plant spacing: 20″ x 20″ (50 x 50 cm).

White Cabbage

100 g white cabbage gives:
32 calories
92 g water
2 g protein
0.2 g fat
5.4 g carbohydrate
60 mg calcium
50 mg phosphorous
0.5 mg iron
25 units of vitamin A
0.07 mg thiamin
0.06 mg riboflavin
0.3 mg niacin
50 mg vitamin C

The white cabbage can, if required, be sown and transplanted early, as it is particularly vulnerable to frost, although there are hardy varieties. It can be planted straight into open ground.

Plant spacing: 20″ x 20″ (50 x 50 cm).

Early white cabbage sometimes splits and cracks if it has grown too quickly. If the heads are not ready for picking, then give them a half turn, to agitate the stem. It is simpler to restrict cultivation to the autumn white cabbage varieties which mature best during the damp autumn weather. They are also better for long-term storage.

White cabbage can be left to grow well into late autumn, but it is as well to crop them before the real frosts start.

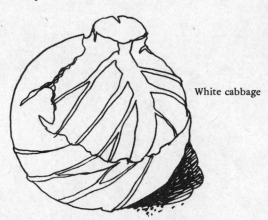

White cabbage

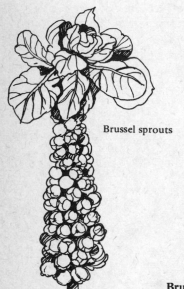

Brussel sprouts

Brussel Sprouts

100 g Brussel sprouts gives:
57 calories
85 g water
4 g protein
0.5 g fat
7.2 g carbohydrate
30 mg calcium
60 mg phosphorous
1.0 mg iron
65 units of vitamin A
0.11 mg thiamine
0.06 mg riboflavin
0.03 mg niacin
80 mg vitamin C

Brussel sprouts are the hardiest variety of cabbage. They are exposed to the same hazards as other related vegetables, but suffer far fewer problems. Sprouts can be sown directly into open ground or transplanted from frames to pots once the hardest frosts are over.

Plant spacing: 2′ x 2′ (60 cm). The small sprouts taste best after a frost which they can resist (even down to −20°C). They can be harvested in the snow — if you have any left, of course!

Sprouts do not demand as nutritious a soil as other cabbages and too much fertilizing can make the heads loose in texture.

Green Cabbage

100 g green cabbage gives:
37 calories
87 g water
3.9 g protein
0.6 g fat
3.7 g carbohydrate
225 mg calcium
60 mg phosphorous
2.2 mg iron
810 units of vitamin A
0.12 mg thiamin
0.35 mg riboflavin
0.8 mg niacin
110 mg vitamin C

100 g red cabbage gives:
22 calories
92 g water
1.6 g protein
0.2 g fat
3.5 g carbohydrate
50 mg calcium
30 mg phosphorous
0.6 mg iron
4 units vitamin A
0.10 mg thiamin
0.06 mg riboflavin
0.03 mg niacin
60 mg vitamin C

100 g savoy cabbage gives:
24 calories
92 g water
2.4 g protein
0.2 g fat
4.6 g carbohydrate
67 mg calcium
54 mg phosphorous
0.9 mg iron
61 units of vitamin A
0.05 mg thiamine
0.08 mg riboflavin
0.3 mg niacin
55 mg vitamin C

The green cabbage is unfortunately not cultivated as much as it should be for its nutritional and vitamin value, although it is simple to grow. It is sown and planted later than other cabbage — in June — otherwise it sheds its leaves early in autumn. Like Brussels sprouts, it resists frost and can be left in the ground throughout the winter. Again, it is tastiest after a frost and is not very demanding of soil, fertiliser or manure. Plant spacing: 20″ x 20″ (50 cm).

Red Cabbage

This is another cabbage that can be harvested during Christmas week. Red cabbage has a long growth period and should be transplanted from frames or pots into warm and sunny ground as soon as the frosts are over. It has, in the main, the same soil requirements as white cabbage. Plant spacing: 20″ x 20″ (50 cm).

Savoys

A hardy cabbage that can remain in the ground even under the snow. Savoys are like white cabbage but have small, buckled, crinkly leaves. They are delicate and tasty.
Plant spacing: 24″ x 20″ (60 x 50 cm).
Similar conditions to white cabbage.

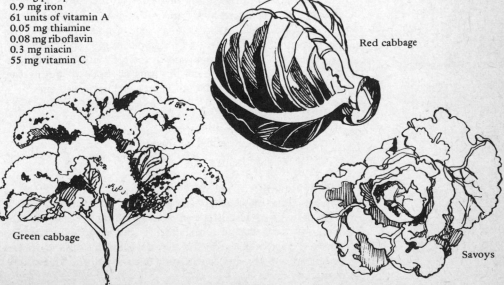

Red cabbage

Green cabbage

Savoys

Chinese Cabbage

100 g chikils gives:
8 calories
93 g water
0.8 g protein
0.1 g fat
1.0 g carbohydrate
35 mg iron
3 units of vitamin A
0.02 mg thiamine
0.03 mg riboflavin
0.2 mg niacin
16 mg vitamin C

Chinese cabbage, or chikils is an old Chinese vegetable that has returned to us after a period of absence. It is somewhat similar in appearance to Swiss Chard and has a taste between that of cabbage and lettuce and is eaten and served up as both a vegetable and a salad. The heads are elongated and the light green leaves are delicate. Chikils is easily cultivated. It need not be sewn until midsummer, otherwise it may bloom before the head has had time to develop fully. Sown into open ground and thinned to 8″–10″ (20–25 cm) spaces. Row spacing 16″ (40 cm). Cultivated like white cabbage. Will grow even in stiff, loamy clay. Growth period: approximately 8 weeks. Harvest before the leaves become large and coarse.

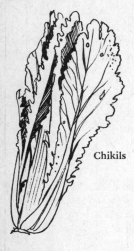

Chikils

Kohlrabi

Kohlrabi

100 g kohlrabi gives:
30 calories
90.1 g water
2.1 g protein
0.1 g fat
46 mg calcium
50 mg phosphorous
0.6 mg iron
0.06 mg thiamine
0.2 mg niacin
61 mg vitamin C

The Kohlrabi is not as much cultivated as it used to be, even though it is an undemanding and easily grown vegetable. It is the thick turnip-like stem that is used; when this has become the size of an apple it is time for harvesting. It should not be bigger or it becomes tough and dry. Cultivated like cabbage, but grows faster. Can be sown in staggered crops in light, warm soil. Row spacing: 16″ (40 cm). Plant spacing: 8″ (20 cm).

Soil requirements for all cabbages
Nutritious, moisture retaining, limey, light, loamy soil is ideal (*pH* value 6.5–7.5).

General plant care for cabbages
Do not cultivate cabbage on the same spot time and time again. This is an important rule, to minimise the risk of club root, which swells the roots and rots them and subsequently causes the spreading of bacteria in the soil. This disease occurs mainly in sour, lime deficient soil, but rarely in well-balanced natural cultivation.

Attack by the *cabbage root fly* can be prevented by sprinkling dry wood ash on and around the stems of young plants (2—3 days after planting). The covering should be thick and tight so that the fly does not get a chance to lay its eggs in the immediate proximity of the cabbage — no eggs are laid in the ash. If the ash rains or blows away, then the procedure should be repeated. Ash is also a general deterrent to fleas and beetles.

There are several ways of resisting the attack of the *cabbage white*. Preventive measures are best. Tomatoes have a more pungent smell than young cabbage. Therefore plant in some tomatoes on your cabbage patch. This will help keep the butterflies at bay, at least until the cabbages mature and give off a stronger smell themselves. Subsequently, hand pick away any larvae and look out for the colonies of yellow eggs that are found on the underside of the leaves.

Black radish planted between the cabbage rows has also proved an efficient protection against all kinds of pests.

The 'tomato method' does not work with red cabbage. Instead, you can try other strong smelling plants that deter cabbage pests — for example, rosemary, sage, thyme, mint . . .

POD BEARING VEGETABLES

Beans

Even if you keep a kitchen garden as a hobby, you cannot ignore the idea of saving by having home-grown crops. Growing beans is a productive use of your energies. 'A hundred to one' — a cliché for French beans — is a conservative estimate, as one bean can produce up to 300 new ones. Beans are also protein rich and vegetarians have a good alternative to meat in beans and peas and, anyway, in a protein deficient world, bean cultivation should be considered an important and useful occupation.

No beans, except broad beans, should be sown before the soil temperature is 10°C, otherwise the plants will rot before they have had the chance to develop.

If you are sure that the frosty nights have passed, then plant out the beans before sprouting, but little is gained by this as they require warmth to grow. It is just as well to wait for the warm weather and then to transplant.

The soil surface should be loose and when the plants are about 4″ in height the soil can be earthed up a little.

Beans are usually divided into three groups: garden beans, broad beans and runner beans. A fourth group should really contain soya beans. The common garden beans are dwarf, french and wax beans and brown beans.

Runner beans

The pods of runner beans are flat and broad and sometimes stringy. They should be cut into strips before boiling. Row spacing 14″ (35 cm). Plant spacing 4″ (10 cm). Runner beans are not particularly fussy about their soil and grow well on either loamy or sandy soil.

French beans

100 g french and green beans gives:
34 calories
90 g water
1.8 g protein
0.2 g fat
6 g carbohydrate
45 mg calcium
35 mg phosphorous
1.1 mg iron
60 units vitamin A
0.08 mg thiamine
0.10 mg riboflavin
0.6 mg niacin
18 mg vitamin C

French beans have round, green non-fibrous pods with thick skins. Like runner and wax beans, they are harvested before they are fully grown and often as very small beans when they are known as haricot verts. Row spacing 16″—18″ (40—50 cm). Plant spacing 4″ (10 cm). (the same with wax and kidney beans).

Wax beans

Like french beans, wax beans have pulpy non-fibrous pods, but they are yellow or cream coloured. They should not be harvested too late if you want the best taste and quality.

Kidney (brown) beans

100 g brown beans gives:
347 calories
11 g water
18.9 g protein
1.7 g fat
61.9 g carbohydrate
100 mg calcium
450 mg phosphorous
70 mg iron
No vitamin A
0.18 mg thiamine
0.30 mg riboflavin
1.7 mg niacin
No vitamin C

These beans should be left to ripen on the plants. When the frost comes, you should uproot the plants and hang them to dry. Later, you can split the pods and take out the dry beans.

Flowerbeans

Cultivated mostly as a decorative plant against a fence or a net, flowerbeans grow quite high: 8 − 10′ and require supports to climb on. They have pulpy, non-fibrous pods that can be used in the same way as French and wax beans.

Broad beans

Broad beans differ considerably from other beans in cultivation requirements. They can be sown earlier and are very accomodating when it comes to soil and plot allocation. They are also frost resistant. If you plant broad beans in a potato patch, they are less vulnerable to attack from the pea and bean weevils. Furthermore, if you crop off the top of the plant as soon as the first pods have developed, further attack is hindered, as it is always in the top of the plant that the weevil lodges itself.

Row spacing: 20″ (50 cm). Plant spacing: 8″ (20 cm).

Soya beans

Soya beans have been cultivated in China for a thousand years and have certainly saved many from starvation and malnutrition. Protein from soya beans is considered as rich as meat protein. In the United States soyas are widely cultivated and it has been suggested that within a decade they will become the most important crop. Also, almost thirty times as much protein is obtained by cultivating soya beans as a direct food source, instead of allowing cows to eat a crop and then using their meat as a food source.

Soya beans require a fairly long growth period and, like other beans, should not be sown before the ground warms up.

Row spacing: 16″ (40 cm). Plant spacing: 2″ (5 cm). Depth 1″–1½″ (3 cm).

The beans are harvested when the leaves turn yellow, or before the frost sets in. Then they can be dried and threshed.

Soil requirements for all beans

All beans flourish best in lime rich, leafy soil with a *pH* value of 7–7.5.

General fertilising

Beans do not like newly fertilised soil. Fertilise with compost the autumn before sowing and lime as required in late winter. Beans, like other pod plants, do not require a lot of extra nitrogen, as their root nodules contain bacteria that convert the free nitrogen from the air into nutritious matter that the plant can absorb. The bacteria in turn obtain their energy from the sugar-rich juice of the plant.

Plant protection for all beans

Bean spot blight is a fungus disease that sometimes occurs in shorter beans, especially if there is too little spacing and the weather is going through a damp spell. Brown spots appear on the leaves, pods and beans. Plants should not be sown too close together in a moist climate and diseased plants should be pulled up and burned.

Pea moth maggots bore small holes in beans. Use high quality seeds and if the soil is not ideal, pre-cultivate them and transplant them once they have gained some strength.

Peas

100 g green peas gives:
86 calories
74 g water
6.3 g protein

In contrast to beans, peas need a certain chill to grow and most types can be readily cultivated in northern climes. As soon as the soil can be worked it is time to sow — first split

0.2 g fat
14.2 g carbohydrate
19 mg calcium
110 mg phosphorous
1.9 mg iron
60 units vitamin A
0.40 mg thiamine
0.02 mg riboflavin
2.1 mg niacin
20 mg vitamin C

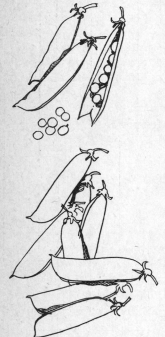

peas, then wrinkled or sugar peas and round peas. One can sow marrowfat peas, together with beans, when the soil has warmed up a bit. Otherwise, the plants rot in the cold soil before they have had time to grow.

With several sowings, you can pick peas from early June to the end of September. The harvest season can be further prolonged by cultivating early, main crop and late pea varieties.

Marrowfat peas

These peas give a richer yield and a better quality than the usually earlier cultivated 'split peas'. They have a delicious flavour and one can boil the whole pod, dip it in butter and extract the peas with one's teeth.

Wrinkled or sugar peas

These belong to the early maturing variety. Growth period about seven weeks. The pods are harvested as soon as they have developed and while they are still thin. Can be sown early.

Split peas

A middle crop variety, between sugar and marrowfat peas. Again, both the peas and the pulp and tender pods can be eaten.

There are many varieties of peas, low, medium and tall. The tall varieties give greater yields, but need a trellis support, such as a net, or something more substantial. The lower varieties are therefore easier to cultivate.

Row spacing for the low variety: 12″ (30 cm), medium: 16″ (40 cm) (use small branches and sticks for support), and the tall variety, double rows 4″ (10 cm) apart and 3′ (90 cm) between the rows. Plant spacing: 2″ (5 cm). Planting depth: 2″ (5 cm). It is prudent to cover the seeds with netting until they have sprouted. When the plants are 4″ (10 cm) tall the soil can be earthed up around them.

Soil requirements for all peas

The ideal is a deep, rich, limey, leafy soil (*pH* value 7.5). The early varieties also grow well in sandy soil, while the later need a more moisture-retaining soil, even clay will do if it is often worked.

Fertilising

Like beans, peas live in harmony with their roots' nitrogen fixing bacteria. Therefore fertilising need only mean some composting in the autumn and some liming, if required, in the late winter. Wood ash can be readily emptied onto the pea beds.

Plant protection for all peas

Pea blight is the equivalent to bean spot blight and is treated in the same way (see p. 43).

The pea moth lays its eggs in the flowers and the yellow/white larvae that are about 2 mm long gnaw holes in the unripened peas.

Thrips are other larvae that turn into black insects and disfigure leaves, flowers and pods. Pods attacked by these larvae first become a silver colour and then turn brown. If an attack has really taken hold, it is best to pull up the plants and burn them.

There are other pests that can reduce pea plants if one is unlucky, but this largely depends, as always, on whether the soil is healthy and alive, the seeds are healthy and the plants are strong enough to resist pests and disease. It is the weakened plant that is attacked.

ONIONS

The honourable old onion can look back, for its origin, to the beginning of history. It is referred to in the Fourth Book of Moses, where the children of Isreal, hanker after some red onions, garlic and leeks to eat, just like they had in Egypt. And what would today's household be without onions, in some form or another — to cook, fry or use raw as a herb in all kinds of dishes, and as a medicine? In ancient times the onion was valued medicinally 'to stimulate urination'. Even modern scientists feel that the onion is of great importance in our diet. Fresh garlic, especially, is supposed to help resist infections and onion oil stimulates blood circulation (all types of onions contain a sulphurous, volatile oil — garlic contains the most).

No garden can be considered complete without some type of onion. The onion is extremely hardy and adjusts itself to most soil and climate conditions.

Yellow (Spanish) and Red Onions

These can be sown very early — by the end of March if they are going to ripen the same year. One can also sow the seeds closely together one year and use small onions as bulbs for the following year (harvested and dried). However, the easiest method is to buy bulbs from a nursery that you know does not use poisons.

100 g onions gives:
36 calories
87 g water
1.4 g protein
0.2 g fat
7 g carbohydrate
32 mg calcium
35 mg phosphorous
0.4 mg iron
4 units vitamin A
0.03 mg thiamine
0.04 mg riboflavin
0.1 mg niacin
10 mg vitamin C

The bulbs are planted in shallow drills 1¼" (3 cm), otherwise they grow long necks. Bulb spacing: about 4" (10 cm). Row spacing: 10"–12" (25–30 cm). To keep the onion fly away, plant carrots in every other row.

When seeds are used, the plants should be thinned to about 4" (10 cm) apart. When the plants are 3"–4" (25–30 cm) high it is a good idea to spread out some wood ash on and around them, after rain or watering. This keeps the pests at bay and also nourishes the soil. Hoe often! If the stalks have not withered by harvest time, break and bend them directly over the onion neck and the onions will mature faster. The onion should be well ripened to keep for a long time.

Onions are hung up for drying: for example in the net bags that oranges are packaged in, or in bunches, They should be stored in a cool, dry place. Onions grown from seeds are smaller, but they generally last better than the bulb-grown larger onions.

Soil requirements

Onions grow well on most soils that are not too dry or lime-deficient. The soil must be hoed frequently, especially in clay conditions. The soil should be neutral (*pH* value 7–7.5).

Fertilising

If you mix in natural fertiliser in the autumn (lime, if necessary, in late winter) and add compost and, for example, blood meal or other organic preparations in the early spring, you ought to get a good harvest, although onions should never be grown in freshly manured soil.

Plant protection

By using crop rotation and healthy soil, the onion is not usually troubled by pests. If the onion fly discovers your onion patch and the small grey larvae become established in any onions, the only thing to do is to dig up the plants, save what you can and burn the rest. However, ash spread on and around the plants will keep the onion fly away, and with carrots sown in alternate rows, the smell of onions deters the carrotfly, so that you discourage both pests at once!

Shallots

The true red or yellow shallots have elongated onion bulbs that are separated in clefts. The clefts should be planted in the soil in the same way as garlic.

Another variety of shallot (or potato onion), is hardier and more suitable to northern climates, where it can replace the red onion, One old bulb will form clusters of new bulbs

around it. Plant spacing should be 8″ (20 cm) and row spacing 14″ (35 cm).

For soil requirements, fertilising and plant protection, refer to the yellow and red onions, above.

Spring onions

Spring onions are sown well spaced and shallow, early in the spring and are not thinned out, unless one wants to use them fresh as spring onions. When the leaves wither the onions are taken up and stored in a dark place, if one wants to keep them white.

Soil requirements

Spring onions, unlike other varieties, prefer a fine tilth and do not need fertilising.

Chives

100 g chives gives.
55 calories
83 g water
3.6 g protein
0.7 g fat
7.6 g carbohydrate
167 mg calcium
75 mg phosphorous
1.3 mg iron
50 units vitamin A
0.14 mg thiamine
0.15 mg riboflavin
0.6 mg niacin
47 mg vitamin C

Chives, which are perennial plants, grow well on all types of soil that are not too dry or impoverished. They are reproduced either by seeding or splitting up clumps early in spring. The flowers are pretty, dried as everlastings.

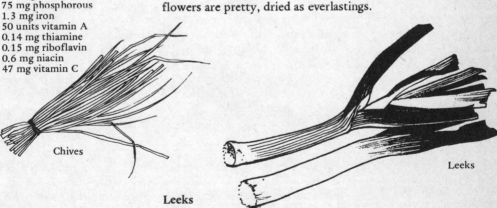

Chives

Leeks

Leeks

100 g leeks gives:
26 calories
90 g water
1.5 g protein
0.1 g fat
4.5 g carbohydrate
60 mg calcium
28 mg phosphorous
2.0 mg iron
55 units vitamin A
0.12 mg thiamine
25 mg vitamin C

If chives, spring onions and shallots do not sound exciting, then leeks should.

Like other onion plants, leeks have been grown since time immemorial. As they have a long growing period, seeds should be sown as early as possible in jiffy pots or under glass. The seedlings are transplanted when they begin to crowd each other and when there is still some spring moisture in the soil. Row spacing: 16″ (40 cm). Plant spacing: 8″ (20 cm).

If you want leeks with pale necks, then you should earth up

the soil around the plants. This can be started three weeks after transplanting.

In most places leeks can be left in the ground during winter, to be harvested the next spring. Do not forget to water your leeks during dry periods — every evening if necessary! Growth time: 150 − 190 days.

Soil requirements

Leeks prefer well drained clay soil and do not like light, sandy soils that do not retain water. Generally, though, they are not very particular.

Fertilising

Composting is most important. Leeks flourish where there is a lot of organic material. Bone and/or fish meal that contains phosphates improves a leek-bed. Fresh fertiliser should not be used.

Plant protection

The same as for red and yellow onions.

Garlic

100 g garlic gives
13 calories
61.3 g water
6.2 g protein
0.2 g fat
30.8 g carbohydrate
29 mg calcium
202 mg phosphorous
1.5 mg iron
0.25 mg thiamine
0.08 mg riboflavin
0.5 mg niacin
15 mg vitamin C

This perennial plant requires a long growth period. The bulbs are divided into cloves and planted just under surface soil, about 4″ (10 cm) apart, as early as possible in the spring. The crop is ready for harvest 150 days after sowing. If not ripe, garlic can be left in the ground during the winter. It is frost hardy and not open to pest attack. For the best results, nutritious soil is needed. Row spacing: 10″ (25 cm).

Both garlic and chives can be planted here and there in the garden, to good effect, as they deter pests — but not amongst peas and beans.

Tree onion

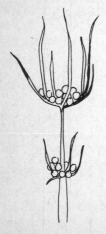

An unfavoured member of the family is the perennial tree onion, which is easily cultivated and fertile year after year. Clusters of small onions are produced on the long stems thrown up from the bulbs, which give the plant an unusual appearance.

In time, these stems and clusters bend towards the ground, where they immediately take root. Therefore it is important to keep the surrounding ground free from weeds, but otherwise the tree onion is not demanding.

The self-propagating tree onion will grow until the summer, when it will produce its own clusters of small onions. Next spring the plants should be taken up and used. One can, of course, also use the smaller onions. They are hardy plants.

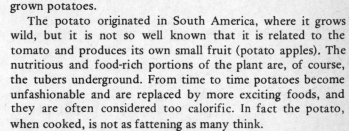

PLANTS WITH TUBERS

Potatoes

100 g potatoes gives:
88 calories
76 g water
2.2 g protein
0.1 g fat
12.9 g carbohydrate
8 mg calcium
42 mg phosphorous
0.7 mg iron
2 units vitamin A
0.10 mg thiamine
0.03 mg riboflavin
1.0 mg niacin
22 mg vitamin C

If you have a patch of ground that will grow things, you shouldn't miss the chance of the delicate taste of freshly grown potatoes.

The potato originated in South America, where it grows wild, but it is not so well known that it is related to the tomato and produces its own small fruit (potato apples). The nutritious and food-rich portions of the plant are, of course, the tubers underground. From time to time potatoes become unfashionable and are replaced by more exciting foods, and they are often considered too calorific. In fact the potato, when cooked, is not as fattening as many think.

It has been discovered that the potato's protein is as good as egg protein. With a 10—15% starch content, the potato is a good energy source, as well as being rich in protein (approximately 2%) and contains vitamins C and B and various minerals, especially potassium.

Different varieties are grown for summer consumption and winter needs.

Early potatoes are planted in mid-March. The later varieties grow more slowly. They can be planted at the same time, or you can wait as late as early May.

Earlier harvests can be obtained if the potatoes are pre-cultivated, e.g. placed in shallow boxes 4—6 weeks before transplanting. The boxes should be placed in a light, though not over-warm place. The roots should be short and strong.

One can also grow early potatoes under black plastic. The plastic is spread out on the ground, and then slit at about 12″ intervals, into which the potatoes are placed and firmly pressed in. They should lie on the soil surface so that they can be easily gathered when mature.

Even with plastic, you should not plant potatoes too deep — about 2″—3 (5—7 cm) below the surface and with about 12″ (30 cm) spacing. Row spacing: 20″ (50 cm). If you expect frost after the leaves have come up, the soil should be earthed up around the plants, or alternatively hay can be used as a covering.

When the plants are 6″—8″ (15—20 cm) high, earth up the soil around the potatoes. This should be done at least once during the growth period.

And so to sowing! It is now fairly difficult in these times of poisonous sprays to find seed potatoes that have not degenerated and are therefore susceptible to diseases and pest attacks. It is impotant to have healthy seed potatoes if you want to harvest a healthy crop of potatoes.

49

Cultivators using biological methods try hard to produce potatoes that are more resistant. Strains such as Grata and Aquila are the result of such work. This year (1973) Grata has given me a fantastic crop of unblemished potatoes.

Other winter potatoes are the *Magnum Bonum* (white and floury), *King Edwards* (somewhat floury) and the *Bintje* (yellow and not floury).

Amongst the earlier varieties the *Arran Pilot, Duke of York, Ulster Chieftan* and *Home Guard* should be mentioned. A new early variety is *Maria*.

Among the later earlies: *Ben Lomond, Great Scot, Pentland Dell*.

Winter potatoes do not need harvesting until the plants have withered. They should be dug up in dry weather and stored in a dry, airy and cool place.

If you are careful to pull out perennial weeds during the early growing season, the potatoes will resist the rest. It is therefore a good idea to grow potatoes one year where you want a weed-free plot for the next year, e.g. for strawberries.

Soil requirements

Healthy, deep soil gives the best quality potatoes, but one can cultivate them on most soils that are not heavy clays or light sands. The soil should not be limed — potatoes prefer acidic soil. (*pH* value 5—6).

There is a big difference between potatoes grown in sandy soil and those grown in clay or peat soils. The former have a characteristic shape to them and are tasty and firm. In peat soils, potatoes tend to be under-developed, tasteless and wet.

Fertilising

Fertilise with natural fertiliser or compost as usual in the autumn, before the growing period. If you feel that more compost should be spread out in the spring, then this should be done at least 14 days before planting.

Do not use sea weed or wood ashes.

Too much nitrogen in your potato patch will give lots of leaves and few potatoes. In addition, the potatoes will blacken when cooked.

Plant protection

Blight: brown and black patches on the shoots which then wither early. It is often the seed potatoes that are infected; therefore, use healthy seed. Sensitive varieties are: Bintje and King Edward. Magnum Bonum is stronger and Grata and Aquila are almost completely resistant.

Brown rot: spores from the blight are spread to the tubers by means of rainwater. Brown patches and brown or grey depressions occur on the potato. If the foilage becomes infected, cut it off and burn it. Do not harvest for at least 14 days afterwards.

Scab: brown, corky scabs on the peel. The soil is too limey.

Wireworms: make holes in the potato and bite off the buds. Do not cultivate potatoes where there has recently been grass. Pick away all visible larvae when working the soil.

Voles: plant broad beans or peas in rows between the potatoes. Broad beans are not usually troubled by greenfly either. This system saves space while keeping voles away.

Fresh potatoes for Christmas: Plant some potatoes fairly deep, in the middle or end of July. Cover with hay or leaves or an upturned box when the frost comes.

Jerusalem artichokes

100 g Jerusalem artichokes gives:
76 calories
79 g water
1.5 g protein
0.2 g fat
16.3 g carbohydrate
30 mg calcium
33 mg phosphorous
0.4 mg iron
0.10 mg thiamine
5 mg vitamin C

The Jerusalem artichoke is related to the sun flower and probably came from North America. It is well worth cultivating as it is very nutritional and, amongst other things, contains inulin, a substance that is used in the production of fruit sugar. It is not demanding of its soil or its setting. It is sown like the potato, with about 12″ (30 cm) between each plant.

Row spacing 28″ (70 cm). Depth of planting 6″ (15 cm). The Jerusalem artichoke should be harvested as late as possible, or left in the ground over winter. In this case, it should be covered with hay or leaves, so that one can harvest when required. It is best to set aside a corner in the garden to cultivate Jerusalem artichokes year after year, otherwise it can become a troublesome weed in the form of discarded tuberous lumps. Earth up around the plant when it is 18″ (50 cm) high. It becomes 6′ (2 m) tall.

Soil requirements

The Jerusalem artichoke grows on almost any soil, but it flourishes, like the potato, on well-fertilised sandy soil on an open, airy patch.

Fertilising

Fertilised like potatoes (see p. 50). In the spring you can mulch in some fishmeal compost, about two weeks before planting.

Plant protection

The Jerusalem artichoke usually keeps itself healthy.

Carrots

100 g carrots gives
38 calories
88 g water
1.0 g protein
0.3 g fat
7.5 g carbohydrate
38 mg calcium
35 mg phosphorous
0.6 mg iron
1200 units of vitamin A
0.06 mg thiamine
0.07 mg riboflavin
0.05 mg niacin
6 mg vitamin C

Carrots were cultivated in Greece and Italy over 2000 years ago: They are easily digested vegetables, rich in vitamin C, and in karotin which our bodies convert to vitamin A.

You should sow very early in the spring as the seeds require a long growth period. Thinning can be started after 70—80 days. You can stimulate the seeds by immersing them in warm water (20°C) for a few days. Then the water should be drained off and the seeds dried before mixing them with some sand and planting them in moist seed beds. Just as with the sowing of parsley, it is a good idea to mix in some quick growing radish seeds, so one knows where the rows lie when working the soil.

For winter needs it is just as well to wait to sow in May or June, otherwise the carrots over-develop and split. Row spacing 12"—18" (30—45 cm) (more for the strong winter carrots). Seeding depth: 1" (2 cm). First thinning to 1" (2 cm) and then up to 4" (10 cm) (for winter carrots especially). Small, buttered spring carrots are a delicious treat. Pick out the largest plants when thinning, as this prolongs the harvesting time.

Carrots are very frost resistant and can be left in the ground over a mild winter (if there are no voles nearby!). You should cover the beds so that the ground doesn't freeze and you can pull up supplies when required. I prefer to harvest in October—November, so I have time to clear up and fertilise, etc. before the winter stillness settles again over my kitchen garden.

Soil requirements

Loose, airy soil, e.g. sand or leafy, loamy soil. Sticky clays is not good for carrots. Neutral, limey soil. (*pH* value 6.5—7)

Fertilising

Do not use newly fertilised soil — then the roots are more susceptible to insect larvae. Lime if necessary, early in spring, or late winter. Refer to the crop rotation table, p. 20. Potassium is necessary for the sugar formation in carrots. Wood ash, seaweed and bracken are good potassium sources.

Plant protection

The carrot has two main enemies: the greenfly that twists and distorts the leaves, and the carrot fly that likes to lay its eggs

in the broken up soil around the thinned plants. The larvae ruin the plants and cause mature carrots to become unusable and partly rotten. Therefore pack down the soil after thinning, or sprinkle sand along the rows. Water and then liberally pour on wood ash so that the plants become dusty. In this way the attacks are deterred, the greenfly does not like a dusty leaf and the carrot fly will not lay eggs on the ash. At the same time you should add potassium. For extra protection, plant or sow onions in alternate rows (see p. 46). There are other strong smelling compounds which deter pests. Fresh wood shavings /sawdust, is another old and well tried remedy. And herbs of different kinds . . .

It is completely unnecessary to spray with strong poisons. How much of these must we already have had to absorb in 50 or 60 years. Beware of imported carrots. In some countries, DDT and other strong poisons are still used against pests.

100 g parsnips gives:
71 calories
83 g water
1.6 g protein
0.3 g fat
15 g carbohydrate
56 mg calcium
75 mg phosphorous
0.6 mg iron
2 units vitamin A
0.1 mg thiamine
0.09 mg riboflavin
0.2 mg niacin
20 mg vitamin C

Parsnips

Parsnips, like carrots, are an historical crop and are the easiest of vegetables to cultivate. They can be sown in the autumn, or very early in the spring. But there is no hurry, either, as they can be sown late or left in the ground over winter. Frost improves their taste. Row spacing: 12—14″ (30—35 cm), through to 4″—5″ (10—12 cm). The 'Student' variety is particularly suitable for the winter. Harvesting should take place when the top of the root has a diameter of 2″—3″ (5—7 cm) — about 120 days after sowing.

Soil requirements

Parsnips grow in all soils that are not too stoney — though they grow biggest (up to 16″ (40 cm) long) in deep, fertile, loamy soil (*pH* value 6.5—7).

Fertilising

Like carrots, parsnips do not like newly fertilised soil. If the soil is deficient, add fish or blood meal 14 days before sowing.

Plant protection

Parsnips are not usually attacked by pests or diseases; however, you should avoid growing them with carrots, for if the carrots are attacked, it is likely that the parsnips will be too.

Radishes

100 g radishes gives:
20 calories
93 g water
1.2 g protein
0.1 g fat
3.5 g carbohydrate
40 mg calcium
30 mg phosphorous
1.4 mg iron
1 unit vitamin A
0.05 mg thiamine
0.04 mg riboflavin
0.1 mg niacin
25 mg vitamin C

Another ancient crop that has spread from the Mediterranean where it has been grown for a thousand years.

Radish seeds grow quickly, even early in spring, and after only 4 weeks the first crop can be harvested. It is sensible to cultivate radishes in a small bed, taking up little room in the garden. The first seeds can be grown amongst carrots and parsnips. If continuous supplies are required, then sow at 14 day intervals in some shady spot. Sparse sowing needs no thinning. Early crops are best, because the secret of crisp, good tasting radishes is in their quick growth. Old radishes become tough and woody.

There are round and elongated varieties. A newcomer is the giant white radish, which I think is a cross between a traditional radish and a black radish. It can be up to 18" (45 cm) long and 2" (5 cm) in diameter when grown under good conditions. A white radish in a carrot form is yet another variety.

Soil requirements

Radishes grow best in soil that does not contain too much organic material. Even if your soil is in poor condition, you can still get good radishes, though they do not like hard, dry stony ground.

Fertilising

Not newly fertilised soil. In case of nutrient-deficient soil, fertilise with bonemeal.

Plant protection

Fleas and midges sometimes attack the leaves in dry conditions, though this is not usually a serious problem.

Black radishes

100 g black radishes gives:
20 calories
93 g water
1.2 g protein
0.1 g fat
3.5 g carbohydrate
40 mg calcium
30 mg phosphorous
1.4 mg iron
1 unit vitamin A
0.05 mg thiamine
0.04 mg riboflavin
0.01 mg niacin
25 mg vitamin C

The black radish is a vegetable that can be cultivated in northern climates. It has a sharper taste than the traditional radish. It is common in Germany and now is being grown more frequently abroad, foremost as a winter radish. It has a black skin and white flesh. It is often used thinly cut on sandwiches, in salads, or grated.

The summer variety is sown as soon as the soil can be prepared; the winter radishes, about midsummer. Row spacing: 10" (25 cm), plant spacing: 3"–4" (7–10 cm). The

black radish is very frost hardy and can be left in the ground well into autumn, though it should not be allowed to grow too large, as this impairs the taste.

Soil requirements and fertilising

The radish is often sown as a second crop, after early potatoes and spring lettuce and the plot needs no further preparation as the radish is not very fastidious.

Swedes

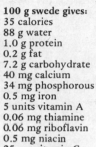

100 g swede gives:
35 calories
88 g water
1.0 g protein
0.2 g fat
7.2 g carbohydrate
40 mg calcium
34 mg phosphorous
0.5 mg iron
5 units vitamin A
0.06 mg thiamine
0.06 mg riboflavin
0.5 mg niacin
25 mg vitamin C

Swedes are related to cabbages. They should be sown, preferably in a shady spot, early in spring. Row spacing: 16″ (40 cm), space after thinning: 8″ (70 cm). Harvest when the diameter of the upper root is about 3″ (7 cm). Larger swedes are tough and taste bitter. Harvesting is possible about two months after sowing. If you want winter supplies, you should sow them in July and harvest in October. The late sown swedes are of better quality for storage.

Soil requirements

Nutritious, somewhat clayey soil. In loose soil, that does not retain water, the swede can be attacked by maggots.

Fertilising

Not newly fertilised soil. The latter sowing can readily be done on early potato or lettuce patches. Add peat or compost if the ground is dry.

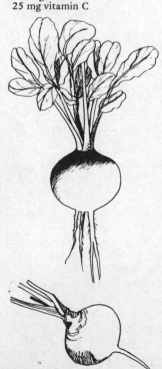

Plant protection

As the swede is related to cabbages, it is open to attack from the same pests: the *cabbage gall weevil* and the *cabbage root fly*, but neither is usually a big problem. The *cabbage white* will avoid cabbage and swede patches if tomatoes or herbs have been planted in between the rows, i.e. sage, thyme, basil. If it is too late, then pick away by hand all cabbage caterpillars. Wood ash around the swedes, or mixed cultivation with beetroots, also keeps away the cabbage rootfly. Sow swedes when you want to get rid of couch grass.

Turnips

In a small garden it may be enough to cultivate either swedes or turnips. Spacing after thinning: 6″ (35 cm). Otherwise, it is cultivated like the swede — perhaps preferring somewhat lighter soil.

Beetroots

100 g beetroot gives:
47 calories
86 g water
1.7 g protein
0.1 g fat
9.5 g carbohydrate
30 mg calcium
40 mg phosphorous
0.8 mg iron
2 units vitamin A
0.03 mg thiamine
0.05 mg riboflavin
0.4 mg niacin
10 mg vitamin C

Beetroots have been cultivated since before the time of Christ. The beetroot is easy to grow and is fairly frost hardy. It is not sown too early: for summer and autumn needs, the middle of May will do. For winter supplies, one should sow around June. Beetroots need 8—10 weeks for full growth and ripening, but you can, of course, harvest continually. Already after the first thinning you can eat the whole plant boiled or fried in butter. Beetroots should not be allowed to grow too large, as they then become tough and fibrous. When the root seems to have a diameter of about 2″ (5 cm) (the neck is usually visible above the ground when ripe), then it is ready to harvest. Row spacing: 14″ (35 cm). After thinning: 6″—9″ (1½—2½ cm).

Soil requirements

Beetroots grow well on most soils in open plots. As they have a shallow root system, soils that retain water are an advantage — a leafy, clay soil, nor must the soil be too acidic. A *pH* value of 6.5—7 will encourage growth.

Fertilising

It is best to use a patch of soil which has not been fertilised for a year. If the soil is too rich, the beetroots become either too big, or they seperate into several roots. A good crop can be gathered where leeks grew the year before.

Plant protection

Flies can attack the small leaves, but this is usually not a serious problem, and new leaves soon replace the damaged ones.

Scorzonera

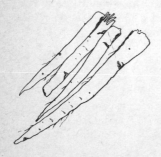

These dark, long thin roots are very nutritious and are a real delicacy with butter or, for example, mushroom sauce. They grow wild in southern Europe and came to the north in the 1700's, where they were first grown for medicinal purposes, then forgotten and are now in favour again. Not even vegetables are free from our fashion consciousness! However, the Scorzonera is well worth its place in the kitchen garden, especially as it is easily cultivated and very frost hardy. The seeds look like pine needles and are easily planted, about 3″—4″ (8—10 cm) apart. In this way thinning is unnecessary.

Row spacing: 14″ (35 cm). Depth: ¾″ (2 cm). Sowing should be done as early as possible as the Scorzonera requires a long growth period: 16–20 weeks.

The roots are ready for harvesting when they are ¾″ (2 cm) in diameter.

They can be left in the ground over winter and if covered with hay, can be taken up as required. Scorzonera is otherwise stored like other root crops, in sand in a cool place. Be careful when taking up and handling them as they are brittle and easily broken. If they are not fully developed, you can leave them in the ground for next year — the scorzonera is perennial — and, of course, becomes much larger. They should, however be harvested before sprouting.

Soil requirements

Deep, nutritious light soil is ideal, but most soils will do.

Fertilising

After the usual autumn fertilising, a little fish or blood meal can be mulched in before sowing.

Plant protection

The scorzonera is seldom attacked by pests or diseases.

Less hardy vegetables

TOMATOES

100 g tomatoes gives:
20 calories
94 g water
1.0 g protein
0.2 g fat
3.4 g carbohydrate
12 mg calcium
24 mg phosphorous
0.5 mg iron
100 units vitamin A
0.07 mg thiamine
0.05 mg riboflavin
0.6 mg niacin
23 mg vitamin C

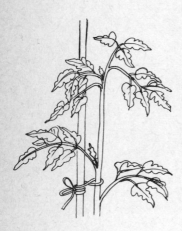

The binding and the prize

Tomatoes, which are related to potatoes, came to Europe from South America in the 1500's and have become popular especially this century when people realised they were rich in vitamins.

Though tomatoes are vulnerable to frost, they can be planted out in the open in front of a warm, sunny wall or fence, even in cold climates. But usually one has to pre-cultivate the crops inside in boxes before transplanting them outside, once the frosts have passed. Plants bought at the market or home-reared should have the bottom flower shoot bloom before transplanting. Care for the plants by moving them into a cooler outhouse (or garage) for one night, before planting them outside. Row spacing: 24". Plant spacing: 16".

Tomatoes need some support, preferably sturdy canes, so as much as possible of the plants are exposed to the sunlight — thus enriching the fruits with vitamins.

After the appearance of the fourth or fifth cluster of flowers you should usually top the plants, 3 or 4 leaves above the highest bunch. All new shoots should be nipped — therefore watch the plant. Tomato bushes, on the other hand, do not need watching or cutting.

Tomatoes grown under good conditions give good yield and, with the possible exception of sun ripe strawberries, there is nothing that gives the gardener greater pleasure than a crop of fresh, red, juicy tomatoes — but the early new potatoes, maybe . . .

I planted seeds from Italian tomatoes; the long narrow variety that are often tinned. Ten plants have grown amongst the cabbage and yielded about 40 lbs of tomatoes. This variety is a little more frost resistant and the fruit has firmer flesh and is not so juicy and full flavoured as the common tomatoes, but it stores well and is an excellent addition to many dishes.

The tomatoes that do not have time to ripen should be put in a cool, dark place. The whole plant can also be taken up and hung in a dark corner of the cellar or garage until the tomatoes have ripened. (You can also pickle green tomatoes.)

If some plants are taken in before the frosts, you can have fresh tomatoes through the winter. If the plants are moved out again next summer, they will blossom again and bear fruit. The plants can be kept in 6″ porous pots once they are transplanted from the boxes. This makes them easy to move.

Soil requirements

Tomatoes will grow on both heavy and light soils, if well drained. The ground must not be too wet or too dry. To prevent drying out, the tomato patch can be covered with black plastic.

Fertilising

Tomatoes like a compost that contains some half decomposed material. After natural fertilising in the autumn and composting in the spring, I usually lay some partially decomposed bracken on the soil when I am going to plant my tomatoes. You could sprinkle ash when you can, naturally! Both the bracken and the ash add potash, which tomatoes need in large quantities. If tomatoes get too much nitrogen, as opposed to potash, the foilage becomes too large in relation to the fruit. Tomatoes appreciate liquid feeding now and again during the growth period.

Plant protection

Tomatoes grown outside are not usually seriously troubled by pests, but tomato diseases have become a problem in the last decade.

Tomato blight: brown patches and streaks on leaves and stems. The infected fruit has a surface depression and the flesh becomes hard and green or green/brown.

Tomato leaf mould: the tops of young leaves and shoots turn yellow.

Brown rot: dark areas and patches form on the stems and the whole plant dries and withers.

Withering through bacterial action: single leaves curl up and wither. Finally the whole plant succumbs and dies.

To combat these, make sure the seeds are from healthy tomatoes and the soil is well prepared with compost. The tomato being a tropical plant requires a lot of warmth and should be planted in a sheltered warm place. Even moisture, covered soil and mixed cropping are further aids. Try also spraying with skimmed milk a few times during the growing season, as well as spraying with horsetail solution.

RED AND GREEN PEPPERS

100 g green peppers gives:
32 calories
90 g water
1.2 g protein

Peppers are another example of the 'newer' vegetables. They are related to tomatoes and require essentially the same treatment for cultivation.

59

0.7 g fat
5 g carbohydrate
11 mg calcium
25 mg phosphorous
0.7 mg iron
100 units vitamin A
0.06 mg thiamine
0.05 mg riboflavin
0.3 mg niacin
150 mg vitamin C

It is best to buy seeds from a nursery to ensure an early crop, rather than relying on seeds taken from a pepper that has been bought to eat. Expose the plants, sown indoors, gradually to the outside, then they can readily be reared in a cold frame, but should be carefully protected from frost.

Soil requirements
The same as for tomatoes.

Fertilising
Peppers do not need as much nutrition as tomatoes — again too much nitrogen favours the foliage at the expense of the fruit. No further fertilising is necessary during the growing period. Leave at least 6—7 fruit pods on each plant — pinch away the others.

Harvesting can take place about 16 weeks after sowing.

Plant care
To my knowledge, peppers have no other enemies than frost.

EGG PLANTS OR AUBERGINES

100 g aubergine gives:
25 calories
92 g water
1.2 g protein
0.2 g fat
4.6 g carbohydrate
13 mg calcium
21 mg phosphorous
0.4 mg iron
5 units vitamin A
0.04 mg thiamine
0.05 mg riboflavin
0.6 mg niacin
5 mg vitamin C

Aubergines are another variety of vegetable that is vulnerable to frost and requires a long growth period — 4½—5 months, and a lot of sun. You should still try your luck with a few plants, even in a cold climate.

If seeds are sown indoors in March then, with a good summer, the fruit should be ready by August. And it is something special to be able to pick tropical fruit in your own garden!

Cultivation requirements are basically the same as those for tomatoes and peppers. Row spacing: 24″ (60 cm), plant spacing: 18″ (45 cm).

The aubergine is a sensitive plant that reacts immediately if it is unhealthy. It is, therefore, necessary to keep a watchful eye out for a thirsty or nutrition-needy plant and also for any indications of pest activity.

CUCUMBERS

Indians are thought to have grown cucumbers since 3000 BC and even in Europe the ancient Greeks and Romans appreciated them. They probably originated in the East Indies.

Cucumbers are very sensitive to frost and should not be planted out until the risk of frost is over.

Gherkins

100 g gherkin gives:
12 calories
96 g water
0.7 g protein
0.1 g fat
1.9 g carbohydrate
17 mg calcium
23 mg phosphorous
0.3 mg iron
25 units vitamin A
0.04 mg thiamine
0.09 mg riboflavin
0.2 mg niacin
8 mg vitamin C

On open ground it is usual to cultivate gherkins — the sort that are pickled in vinegar and salt. They need a lot of space, but one or two plants will produce large yields.

Gherkins should be planted in front of a south-facing wall or preferably nursed in a frame or greenhouse.

Row spacing outside: at least 3′ (1 m). Plant spacing: 10″ (25 cm).

For an early crop, some plants can be left in the frames, if they can be allowed to spread out.

Gherkins need a lot of moisture. During sunny, dry weather the plants should be watered daily.

Gherkins are 96% water, so you can understand how they must crave for it.

Gherkins take about 12 weeks to mature and should be gathered before they start to yellow of bud.

Soil requirements
Leafy, limey clay (*pH* value 7—7.5).

Fertilising
Cucumbers need well fertilised soil. Use natural fertiliser as usual in the autumn and then compost well in the spring. Cucumbers like soil that is rich in organic material.

Plant protection
Radishes and cucumbers grow well together. Cucumbers are not usually troubled by pests and diseases when cultivated on open land.

Ridge cucumbers

Ridge cucumbers can be cultivated on open land, if they have first been in a frame or inside and the summer is warm and long. To taste really good and not bitter, this cucumber requires well fertilised soil, with the right *pH* value and it must never be allowed to become dry. To a large extent, it needs the same conditions as other cucumbers, though it is more sensitive to a lack of care in cultivation, whereas other varieties will usually grow quite well anyway.

Squash

100 g squash gives:
4 calories

Summer squash has only recently been cultivated in Britain. Squash, like cucumber, is very sensitive to frost and cannot be

91 g water
1.1 g protein
0.1 g fat
5.5 g carbohydrate
44 mg phosphorous
22 mg calcium
0.8 mg iron
326 units vitamin A
0.05 mg thiamine
0.07 mg riboflavin
0.5 mg niacin
9 mg vitamin C

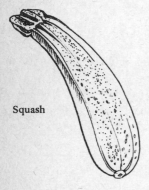

Squash

planted out until all risk of frost is over — but after this, it grows quickly. The plant produces fruit at an unbelievable rate, one larger than the others. The largest specimen from my garden this year weighed about 6 lbs.

Squash of up to 1 lb can be used as a normal ridge cucumber. Larger ones can be fried in strips or chopped up if preferred. It can also be cooked in larger pieces or made into ratatouille, (squash, onion, green pepper, tomato, aubergine).

Seven plants have given me over 200 lbs of squash this year (a rewarding harvest for Middle Sweden, from so little work).

Cultivated basically in the same way as cucumber.

Plant spacing: 32″ x 32″ (80 cm).

Marrows

Like other cucumbers, the marrow needs organically rich soil. Therefore it is sometimes planted on not fully decomposed compost heaps. Row spacing on open ground: 60″ (150 cm). Plant spacing 20″ (50 cm). Other requirement: the same as for cucumbers.

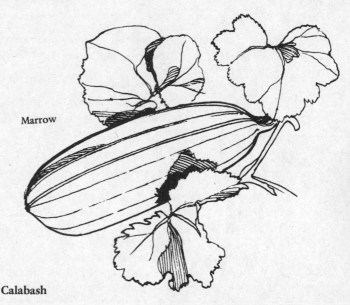

Marrow

Calabash

The calabash is a relation of the marrow. It needs warmth and has a certain curiosity value. The large fruits can be used as bottles, bowls, pots, etc, after the flesh has been scraped out and the skin dried.

Cultivated like the marrow, but requires a warm wall to climb on.

Melon

Melon

Melon needs a lot of sun. But one can rear some plants indoors and transplant them in a cold frame where they can remain the whole summer. Alternatively, if you have a cooler summer they can be grown exclusively in a warm frame.

Melon plants must not be allowed to dry out. During cool summer development can be encouraged by keeping the top of the frame closed. The vines can be topped if they grow too long, and some of the side-shoots can be thinned away.

Soil requirements, fertilizing and plant protection
The same as for cucumbers.

100 g melon gives:
24 calories
94 g water
0.6 g protein
0.1 g protein
0.1 g fat
5 g carbohydrate
18 mg calcium
20 mg phosphorous
0.6 mg iron
100 units vitamin A
0.06 mg thiamine
0.04 mg riboflavin
0.8 mg niacin
30 mg vitamin C

CORN

Sweet corn

Even though corn takes up quite a lot of space and needs lots of nutrition for what it gives, it would be a pity to oust it from the vegetable garden.

It is fun and exciting to cultivate and there is a big difference in the taste of home-grown sweetcorn and that bought in shops.

Sweetcorn is an old crop from South America. It needs a warm and sunny patch on which to grow.

You can sow in pots or a frame and transplant to a sheltered plot once the risk of frost is over. Smaller crops can be planted in a rectangular row. This encourages fertilization. The male flower is found at the top of the cob, the female becomes a spadix in the leaf fold.
Row spacing: 3″. Plant spacing: 20″.
Water in dry weather.

100 g corn gives:
102 calories
74 g water
3.7 g protein
1.2 g fat
20.5 g carbohydrate
9 mg calcium
114 mg phosphorous
0.5 mg iron
No vitamin A
0.15 mg thiamin
0.12 mg riboflavin
1.7 mg niacin
12 mg vitamin C

When the silks at the top of the cobs begin to turn brown then the cob is ready for harvest. The cobs should be firm and stubby. You should part the sheath to make sure the corn is yellow and ripe. If a grain is pressed, a white juice should spurt out. A harvest should yield 4 or 5 cobs per plant. Use the cob as soon as possible after picking, otherwise they become hard and tough.

Growth period from sowing to harvest is 12—15 weeks.

Soil requirements

Deep, nutritious soil, mixed with sand gives the best results.

Fertilizing

Compost, and again compost, Corn likes a lot of organic material in the soil. Use natural fertilizers as usual in the autumn. In the spring, add bloodmeal, bonemeals, Algomin or other organic additives, together with compost.

Plant protection

No problem.

CHICORY

100 g chicory gives:
24 calories
93 g water
1.7 g protein
0.1 g fat
4 g carbohydrate
80 mg calcium
1.2 mg iron
200 units vitamin A
0.07 mg thiamin
0.10 mg riboflavin
0.3 mg niacin
13 mg vitamin C

To cultivate chicory is fun and worthwhile, even if it demands a bit of work.

Sow in frames, or on open land, as early as possible as the seeds are slow growing. Row spacing: 14″ (36 cm). Plant spacing: 8″(20 cm). Water whenever dry.

When frosty nights begin, you should take up the whole plant, cut away the excess foliage and clean up the roots, and then transplant them in a box with peat soil, until about two weeks before Christmas, when forcing can begin.

The roots are placed in half-filled buckets or large pots of peat mould, with holes in the bottom for draining of excess water. Water, and fill with dry mould or fine sand almost to the top. Put the plants in a warm, dark place for "blanching" and continue to water when necessary. After about three weeks, you can cut off the small base and have the most delicious Christmas salad.

Soil requirements and fertilising

The same as for other salads.

Plant protection

No problem.

CELERIAC

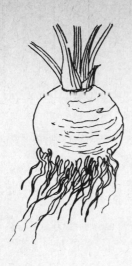

Celeriac came to Europe in the 1700s, after being grown in Egypt since ancient times.

Its cultivation requires time and patience. It has a long growth period and should be sown indoors or in a warm frame as early as March. The correct nursery temperature is 18°–20°C. After the young plants have become strong, they can be planted out at the end of May. Row spacing: 18″ (45 cm). Plant spacing: 12″ (30 cm). Once the plants have taken, they grow fast. Celeriac is quite frost hardy and by October/November, the root can be taken up and put in boxes for winter supply.

Soil requirements

Celeriac needs deep, nutritious, leafy soil (*pH* value 6—6.5) — quite sour soil

Fertilising

In addition to mixed in fertiliser, the transplanted celeriac needs organic fertiliser as well. Algomin, bone meal, meat meal, etc. — at least one supply of such fertiliser is required during the growing season.

MUSHROOMS

Not even the person without the smallest patch of soil, who rents a flat in a tower block, need put his green thumb in his pocket. He can cultivate mushrooms. They can be sown on the balcony, in a dark cellar, in a frame or on open land. All instructions come with the seed packets bought at the nursery or the garden shop.

Perennial vegetables

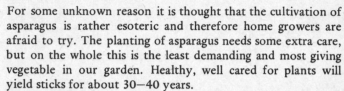

ASPARAGUS

100 g asparagus gives:
16 calories
93 g water
2.1 g protein
0.1 g fat
1.5 g carbohydrate
17 mg calcium
56 mg phosphorous
0.7 mg iron
23 units vitamin A
0.14 mg thiamine
0.09 mg riboflavin
0.8 mg niacin
26 mg vitamin C

For some unknown reason it is thought that the cultivation of asparagus is rather esoteric and therefore home growers are afraid to try. The planting of asparagus needs some extra care, but on the whole this is the least demanding and most giving vegetable in our garden. Healthy, well cared for plants will yield sticks for about 30—40 years.

Known certainly in the third century, asparagus was introduced to Northern Europe in the 1600s. It grows wild in South Eastern Europe.

White asparagus is commonly grown in Britain. The green asparagus (if the shoots are allowed to grow above the ground, they become green), which is more usual in the U.S.A., is richer in Vitamin C and has a more typical asparagus taste.

30—40 plants are enough for household needs. Male plants give larger yields than female plants. The illustrations below show how to plant and look after asparagus. The earliest harvest should be two years after planting. Asparagus can be picked morning or evening, up until midsummer, with the help of a special knife. During the first two harvest years, you should stop picking early. During the years before harvest, you can grow other smaller vegetables between the asparagus rows: radishes, lettuce, parsley, etc. Keep the soil loose, throughout the growth period.

In the autumn, when the leaves go yellow, you should cut them back to a little above ground level.

Plant early in the spring, preferably 2 year old plants. Dig 12" (30 cm) deep trenches about 5' (150 cm) apart.

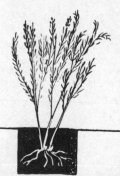

Lay fully decomposed compost in a lump on the bottom of the trench. Plant at 20" (50 cm) intervals. The tip or crown of the asparagus should be 4" (10 cm) below ground level.

For the first year after planting you should cover up the asparagus border early in the spring — by pouring light soil or fine sand over the plant until there is a 4" (35 cm) high bank.

After picking off all the sticks, even out the soil, fertilise, and a 3' (1 m) high bush will grow up.

Soil requirements

Asparagus will grow well enough on all soils, providing they are well drained. The ideal is nutritious, stone-free, leafy, limey, sandy soil in a sunny place. (*pH* value 7—7.5)

Fertilising

For plentiful yields asparagus needs to be well fertilised. Cover the growing area with natural fertiliser and good compost each autumn. Lime in late winter if necessary.

Plant protection

Asparagus usually escapes the attention of pests and diseases. In moist conditions certain varieties can be attacked by rust — brown or orange spots on stems and leaves. Best are preventive measures — to cultivate rust-resistant varieties!

FENNEL

100 g fennel gives:
28 calories
90 g water
2.8 g protein
0.4 g fat
5.1 g carbohydrate
100 mg calcium
51 mg phosphorous
2.7 mg iron
3500 units vitamin A
31 mg vitamin C

Fennel is another of the newer vegetables to Anglo-Saxons, but very common in Italy. It is a vegetable with a fresh, sharp taste, that can be readily cultivated in the more northern climates. You must first sow Fennel in a frame or pots before planting it on open ground in May or June, when all risk of frost should be over. Row spacing: 20″ (50 cm). Plant spacing: 8″ (20 cm). Fennel is perennial and the fruits are used as a fragrance in bread. Earth up soil around the lower part of the stem and leaves a couple of times during the growth period. For fennel to survive the winter unharmed, cover the ground with leaves, or hay.

According to the medical books, the cooked juice of fennel improves the eyesight.

Soil conditions

Warm, sunny spot. Leafy, clay soil that retains moisture.

RHUBARB

100 g rhubarb gives:
11 calories
95 g water
0.5 g protein
0.1 g fat
2.0 g carbohydrate
40 mg calcium

The rhubarb clump, with 3 or 4 crowns for normal household requirements, should be planted in a sunny, warm and undisturbed corner of the garden, so that you can harvest the crisp stalks early in the spring.

Plant spacing: about 3′ (1 m).

20 mg phosphorous
0.3 mg iron
4 units vitamin A
0.02 mg thiamine
0.03 mg riboflavin
0.1 mg niacin
13 mg vitamin C

Do not harvest the first year and be sparing the second, so that the plant has time to develop a mature root system.

Rhubarb grows wild in Mongolia. In Sweden it has been cultivated for a hundred years. In Europe, it was used as a medicine as early as the 1500s.

Soil requirements
Deep and nutritious clay soil is ideal.

Fertilising
Rhubarb is one of the most nutrition-craving vegetables. The reward for lots of natural fertilizer and compost each year is healthy plants growing decade after decade on the same spot.

Forcing
If you want rhubarb really early in the spring, then some roots should be taken up and placed in a deep box or bucket and covered with light, moist soil and put in a dark, warm place.

HORSE RADISH

100 g horse radish gives:
87 calories
74.6 g water
3.2 g protein
0.3 g fat
19.7 g carbohydrate
140 mg calcium
64 mg phosphorous
1.4 mg iron
0.07 mg thiamine
81 mg vitamin C

The horse radish could also be included as a herb, as it is mainly used as such. It originates from Russia and through monastery gardening came to the West, again first as a medicine. When sailors went down with scurvy as a result of vitamin C deficiency, horse radish was used as a cure, even though its vitamin content was not understood at that time. It is also thought to lower blood pressure.

As a medicine, horse radish has been superseded, but it contains pungent oils that still secure its reputation as a tasty herb.

Horse radish grows wild, but if you want to use the roots, then it is best to cultivate it in a certain place, otherwise it can spread out quickly.

About 10″ (25 cm) long root lengths can be planted early in the spring. They should be laid in a furrow and covered with 3″ (8 cm) soil. Once, or preferably two, times during the summer the horse radish should be taken up and cleaned with, for example, a rag, so that the shoots that have sprouted are broken off, except one on the upper part of the root length, which can remain with the roots that have grown out of the original root length.

A perfect horse radish is 12″− 16″(30−40 cm) long and up to 2″ (3 cm) in diameter.

Soil requirements
Deep and rich clay soil.

ANAGALLIS (not mixed)

Livingstone daisy

Godetia

Nemesia

Allyson

Gazania

Petunia

Mimula ?

Sweet peas

Spr Onions
Broad Bean —
French Bean
Beetroot
Carrot
Kale
Lettuce
~~Courgettes~~
Peas — Greenfelt
Potatoes — Early + Main
Tomatoes
+ Super
Manure

Courgettes
Parsnips
Runner Bean

...and now to the heart's delight

HERBS

Northern summers with many hours of daylight are very suitable for the cultivation of herbs. Their aroma becomes stronger.

Kitchen plants were grown as herbs in nordic countries even in Viking times. There was a "herb patch", "nut patch", "cabbage patch" and "nettle patch". A number of varieties of herbs were brought north in the middle ages, by monks from more southerly latitudes.

You do not need a large patch to start a herb garden — even a window box on a sunny balcony will do to start with or, as a last resort, they can be grown in pots indoors. The cultivation of herbs can become an absorbing hobby and the planning of a herb patch can be an interesting winter occupation, while waiting for the spring's more concrete and soil bound tasks.

Harvest and drying

It is important to know which part of the plant should be picked and used. In some cases the seeds are used; in others the leaves, flowers or roots.

Most are harvested by cutting off whole plants, which are rinsed and hung up in sprigs or bunches — beside the stove, if they are to be used immediately. If they are to be dried for future use, then they should be placed in an *airy*, warm and dry spot. When dry, you break off the leaves and flowers and crumble them between your fingers, before putting them into airtight jars.

If it is the seeds that are required, then tie a paper bag around the sprigs so that the seeds are caught as they fall after ripening.

It is also possible to deep freeze herbs, but I prefer drying, except in the case of dill, and possibly tarragon.

When to harvest?

Choose a sunny morning when the day has become dry and the plants' flowers have begun to open. Then the plant is full of the volatile oils we want.

If only the plants' leaves are to be picked, then this should be done just before flowering.

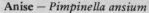

Anise — *Pimpinella ansium*

Annual. About 24″ (60 cm) high.

A rather exacting oriental herb that needs a lot of sun. The seeds are picked in August and used primarily as a spice in the making of rye bread.

"Helps the wind on its way" says an old maxim. Row spacing: 14″ (35 cm). Plant spacing: 8″ (20 cm).

Basil — *Ocimum basilicum*

Annual. About 36″ (1 m) high.

Originates from India.

It is used, for example, to spice soups and sauces, and it is sprinkled on freshly cut tomatoes — and generally used for all tomato dishes. Basil is also one of the 200 herbs that goes into making the monks' special liquer, chartreuse.

The plants grow slowly and it is a good idea to nurse them indoors and then plant out when the frosts have passed.

Row spacing: 10″ (25 cm). Plant spacing: 8″ (20 cm).

Heart's delight — *Melissa officinalis*

Perennial. About 24″ —36″ (60 cm—1 m) high.

Easily grown, and the leaves have a lovely, fresh lemon taste. Can be used in tea and as a spice to salads and sauces.

An historical medicine, thought to strengthen the nerves, improve the memory, prolong youthfulness and prevent hardening of the arteries. A rush to buy seeds?

Row spacing: 12″ (30 cm). Plant spacing: 12″ (30 cm).

Tarragon (French). — *Artemisia dracunculus*

Perennial. About 32″ (80 cm) high.

A fairly hardy plant. The leaves and young shoots are used, fresh or dried, in sauces, vinegar and in mixed herbs.

The simplest method is to buy plants — two are enough. If more are required later, the originals can be divided (after some years).

Row spacing: 24″ (60 cm). Plant spacing: 24″ (60 cm).

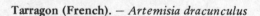

Fennel — *Foeniculum vulgare*

Perennial, when under cover. About 36″ (1 m) high.

Fennel has already been described as a vegetable on page 67. One can also use the seeds as herbs — often as an ingredient in bread. The seeds will not have time to ripen in cold conditions, however.

Borage — *Borago officinalis*

Annual. About 30" (75 cm) high.

An easily grown plant that survives on the poorest soil. You must sow early — growth is slow. You can even sow in Autumn, or nurse the plants indoors and plant out in May. Row spacing: 16" (40 cm). Plant spacing: 16" (40 cm).

The plant propogates very easily.

Both the leaves and the flowers are used; the blue flowers in salad or as a sweetener in baking; the leaves in salad, in tea, or like spinach early in the spring.

"Strengthens the heart".

You should sow borage if you want to attract bees to your garden.

Hops — *Humulus lupulus*

Perennial. About 8'–10' (2½–3½ m) high. Needs a trellis.

Goes into beer, of course, but hops are also a good mixture for helping sleep. The female plants have small yellow/green flower pods that contain lupulin, which gives out that lovely hop aroma.

Hops are very easily grown, happy in sun or shade and fairly hardy.

Hyssop — *Hyssopus officinalis*

Perennial. 24" (60 cm) high.

A well-known historic medicinal plant and herb; bushy, with pretty deep blue flowers. It was formerly used against colds, but now is most used as an ornamental and anniversary flower.

Sown early on open ground. Row spacing: 16" (40 cm). Plant spacing: 20" (50 cm).

Hyssop prefers light, warm soil.

Coriander — *Coriandrum sativum*

Annual. About 20" (50 cm) high.

Coriander is grown mainly for its seeds, although the leaves can be used in soups and sauces. This plant will not contribute to the sweet fragrance of your herb garden — it smells awful. But the dried, ripe seeds give a wonderful orange-like fragrance. They are used in curries.

The Coriander is not particular about its soil and can be sown directly into the ground in May. Harvest in September when the fruits are brown. Row spacing: 20" (50 cm). Plant spacing: 12" (30 cm).

Caraway — *Carum carvi*

Biennial. About 20″ (50 cm) high.

Caraway grows wild, but when cultivated has a stronger taste.

It is mainly the seeds that are used in bread, cheese and snapps, amongst other things. The leaves can also be used, for example, in salads.

Caraway is very easily grown and reproduces itself once it has been established in the garden. As it is a biennial plant seeds can only be gathered in the second year.

Sow in May or the beginning of June.

Row spacing: 18″ (46 cm). Plant spacing: 6″ (15 cm).

Caraway used to always be found in the medicine cupboard. A warm water preparation was said to ease mucus congestion and caraway oil on the stomach was said to help against "pain caused by wind"

Angelica — *Angelica archangelica*

Biennial. About 6′ (2 m) high.

Angelica is a hardy plant — it grows well on highland moors.

Sow as early as possible and thin out to intervals of 20″ (50 cm).

Flowers in late summer but as soon as the stem has grown it should be harvested, cut into sections and boiled as a vitamin-rich brew.

Row spacing: first year 2′ x 2′, (60 cm), second year: 5′ x 5′ (1½ m)

Winter savory — *Satureja montana*

Perennial (there is also the annual summer savory). About 6″–14″ (15–35 cm).

The leaves are used fresh or dry in pea soup, sausage and meat dishes. It has a strong taste and one should be sparing with this herb.

Winter savory can be cultivated on open land if it is sown in April, but it is easiest to buy the plants you need. Plant with 15″ (37 cm) spacing between the rows and 12″ (30 cm) between the plants. Harvest when in full bloom.

Chervil — *Anthriscus cerefolium*

Annual. About 16″ (35 cm).

A solution of chervil leaves, cooked as a soup, can rival the spring's first nettle soup as a taste sensation. The leaves can also be finely chopped and sprinkled over salad, used in spiced butter, or as a decoration in the same way as parsley. It is easily cultivated and grows well everywhere.

Row spacing: 16″ (40 cm). Plant spacing: 10″ (25 cm).

Can be harvested throughout the summer.

Spanish chervil (Myrrhis odorata) is perennial and cultivated in the same way.

Old farm traditions held that chervil helped sleep and alleviated headaches. Linnaeus thought the leaves cleansed the blood.

Lavender — *Lavandula officinalis*

Perennial. About 24″ (60 cm) high.

Lavender makes no great demands, as long as it does not have to withstand too much moisture in the winter, when it can be killed by frosts. It needs a lot of sun, but prefers light soil, so that the small blue, fragrant flowers become intensely coloured and pungent.

It can be sown outside early in spring, or better still, inside for transplanting later.

Row spacing: 16″ (35 cm). Plant spacing: 10″ (25 cm).

When the flowers have just bloomed, they are cut off and hung in bouquets for drying. Lavender blooms at the end of July.

Early in spring, you should prune the plants right down so they become fuller and more attractive.

Lovage — *Levisticum officinale*

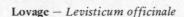

Perennial. About 6′ (2 m) high.

Sometimes called the Maggi variety as the first consomme soups were made with an extract from the Lovage. Monks grew it in their cloister gardens as a medicine against coughs and even plague!

It is not particular about soil or sunshine and is hardy enough to grow throughout Britain.

It is best to buy plants and then plant them, preferably in the spring; but not in the middle of the herb garden, as they can become as tall as a man if they flourish.

The whole plant can be used.

Wormwood — *Artemisia absinthum*

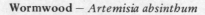

Perennial. 3′ (1 m) high.

A medicinal plant and an important ingredient in absinthe. Moreover, it is so beautiful that a few clumps in the herb garden are certainly worthwhile.

Sweet Marjoram — *Origanum majorana*

Annual. 6″−8″ (15−20 cm) high.

One of the most commonly used herbs. It is good with all vegetables and salads and with most meat and many fish dishes. The Italian pizza herb, origano, is such a close relation to marjoram that you can hardly tell the difference. In south Sweden, marjoram can be sown directly into open ground, but in colder conditions it is best to nurse the small plants before transplanting after the frosts have passed.

Row spacing: 10″ (25 cm). Plant spacing: 6″−8″ (15−20 cm).

Marjoram requires a lot of sunshine, but otherwise is not demanding. The buds and leaves can be picked throughout the year.

Mint — *Curly mint. Mentha crispa. Peppermint. Mentha piperita*

Perennial. About 16″ (40 cm) high.

Mint, usually peppermint, is used in tea and also in mint sauce for lamb and mutton.

Plant spacing: 12″ (30 cm). Be careful that the mint plants don't spread and choke other plants.

Nip off the green shoots during the summer, as required. For drying purposes, the mint should be picked before it flowers — after which the spicy taste quickly weakens.

Common Burnet — *Pimpinella saxifraga*

Perennial. About 18″ (35 cm) high.

Formerly used as a herb in red wine. In the Middle Ages it was known as a medicine against plague, amongst other things. Now it is used for sore throats, catarrh and as a tonic.

It grows wild on dry pastures in Scandinavia. Certainly some Burnet can be planted in the herb garden.

Tansy — *Tanacetum vulgare*

Perennial. 3′ (1 m) high.

A wild and pretty herb that is an interesting addition to the herb garden. It is still used medicinally as a worm repellent agent. It was mainly the flowers that were formerly used against ailments, but now the tansy is used mostly for dyeing textiles.

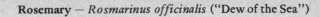

Rosemary — *Rosmarinus officinalis* ("Dew of the Sea")

Perennial. About 5′ (1¾ m) high.

Rosemary is a green bush that grows wild along the Mediterranean coast. It can be kept outdoors during the winter in parts of the country where it is not too cold; elsewhere some protection with straw is usually necessary. In severe winters the plants may be lost and it is advisable to have a small plant potted up and kept indoors.

Rosemary requires a sunny spot, but otherwise is undemanding. Row spacing: 12″ (30 cm). Plant spacing: 8″ (20 cm), on the nursery bed. When moved to a permanent position, plant them 3′ x 3′ (1 m). The leaves can be used fresh, or dried as a spice for meat dishes and also in tea.

Sage — *Salvia officinalis*

Perennial. About 20″ high.

Bushy with soft, grey-green leaves and fragrant blue-violet flowers. The leaves, which can be picked late into winter, can be used fresh or dried in meat dishes or tea.

Sage can be sown directly into sunny, open ground, as early as possible.

Row spacing: 24″ (60 cm). Plant spacing: 20″ (50 cm).

Like lavender and rosemary, sage prefers light, airy soil. The plants are cut back each year to encourage new growth and should be split and replanted every three years.

Sage survives the cold well, but in extreme conditions, it needs covering in winter, to be on the safe side.

Thyme — *Thymus vulgaris*

A perennial bush. About 10″ (25 cm) high.

Thyme was already known as a healing plant in Ancient Egyptian times and is still used as an ingredient in some cough mixtures. Now it is mainly used as a herb, in meat and fish dishes, in soups, in sausages, with vegetables . . . Thyme prefers sunny, dry and sandy soil to grow in. It is sown early in spring, directly into open ground, though again, in severe conditions it is best to nurse the plant indoors or in frames. Row spacing 16″ (40 cm). Plant spacing: 16″ (40 cm). The leaves should be picked just before the plant flowers, and then dried or frozen.

Rue — *Ruta graveolens*

Perennial. About 20″ (50 cm) high.

An old healing and herb plant. Bushy, with leaves that are used in salads and in sandwiches.

It is simplest to buy the plants and then set them out. Two plants are enough.

Southernweed — *Artemisia arbrotanum*

Perennial. About 4′ (120 cm) high.

A traditional herb, with grey-green beautifully fragrant foliage. Mainly used as a spice in strong drinks. Easiest to buy and then plant. One is enough.

Soil requirements for herbs in general

The soil in the herb garden should preferably be light, sandy and on the dry side. A sunny rather than a shady position, will enhance taste and smell.

Berries

STRAWBERRIES

100 g strawberries gives:
39 calories
90 g water
0.8 g protein
0.6 g fat
7.3 g carbohydrate
25 mg calcium
25 mg phosphorous
0.7 mg iron
6 units vitamin A
0.03 mg thiamine
0.07 mg riboflavin
70 mg vitamin C

Nowadays, you can buy fresh strawberries most of the year round. None, however, can compare with the sun-ripened strawberries that can be picked early in the morning for breakfast.

Strawberries have been cultivated in Europe since the eighteenth century, when the cross-fertilizing of the north and south American plants resulted in the *Fragaria* variety. Cultivation has since spread and experiments with new varieties have continually been carried out.

Strawberries can be grown in most parts of the British Isles. Some varieties actually prefer and yield more in areas of lower summer temperatures.

Planting should preferably be done in August. The growing plot must be kept free from perennial weeds that would be difficult to get rid of later.

The first year after planting gives the greatest yields. After even three years the yield can drop, through the spreading of weeds and diseases that attack the weakened plants.

A new strawberry patch should be laid every third/fourth year. For replanting, runners from strong, healthy plants should be used. If it is a bit late, it is better for the runners to be transplanted in early spring instead. These spring strawberries give their best yields the following summer.

Plant spacing: 18″ x 18″ (45 cm) or for easier picking and care, 18″ (45 cm) between the plants and 32″ (80 cm) between the rows.

You should usually cover the surrounding earth with wood shavings, hay, dry grass, etc. to prevent the berries from becoming soiled. Black plastic can also be used and can be bought in packet form for small sized crops. Before laying out the plastic and plants you should earth up the soil into 8″ wide drills. The strawberries are then planted through holes in the plastic. Further holes, 4″ apart, can be made with an awl, for example, to let rainwater percolate through.

The plastic helps the ground to retain its moisture longer — strawberries cannot stand dry soil — and the fruit is protected from the soil as well. A covering of hay, etc. might still be needed to protect the strawberries from coming into direct contact with the hot plastic during a sunny spell.

Views differ on this method of cultivation, which can also be used for growing potatoes, amongst other crops. It is said that the soil dries out within two years, because it is not exposed to the same precipitation as uncovered soil. I usually loosen the plastic and fold back the edges in late autumn and then in spring, fasten them down again with a covering of soil. I have not experienced any other problems. But I have got berries as large as medium sized potatoes, when my neighbours crop has dried up! The strawberry patch should not be a windy place that could move the supports and weights of the plastic and thus make it flap and rip.

When the autumn cold comes, most varieties stop growing and the "winter rest" starts. The "vegetating" stage begins with the spring's light and warmth when the leaves and buds that have previously formed stretch themselves and break out. This stage is over by about the middle of July. Then the plant goes into a "neutral" stage, when roots and shoots are built up. The flower buds are established under the "generative" stage which begins at the end of August.

You should be careful in your choice of plant and respective nursery. Only those that at least *look* healthy should be planted. Some parasites are so small that they are not visible to the naked eye. Firm, dark berries with a sour fresh taste make the best juice and jam.

Soil requirements

Strawberries can grow on most soils, but best results are on well-drained, moisture retaining, sand mixed, leafy soil. Ideal *pH* value 6—6.5.

Fertilising

Strawberries do not need a lot of nutrition. If you use natural fertilizer before planting and add compost soon after autumn picking, then this will be enough for the lifespan of the strawberry patch. Plants are particularly grateful for compost that improves soil structure and stimulates the micro life in the soil.

Plant protection

In healthy soil and by moving the strawberry patch every third or fourth year, homegrown strawberries do not usually suffer from disease.

Naturally, there are some enemies:

Slugs and snails can, in damp conditions, eat the berries. For prevention, see p. 30.

The strawberry beetle, about 1/10th" (3 mm) long is a metallic blue beetle that lays its eggs in the flower-buds and then bites them off. These pests are hard to get rid of, and if the whole crop is affected then you should perhaps use pyrethrum or derris (see p. 31).

Grey Mould is a fungus disease which occurs in warm, damp weather conditions. Different varieties of strawberries have different resistance levels (see p. 78). Do not plant vulnerable varieties too close together. Never fertilize with nitrogen in the spring.

Good results have been obtained in the USA and Holland against both pests and grey mould by cultivating a Mexican plant, *Tagetes minuta*, with the strawberries. The roots secrete a compound which the pests and fungi cannot tolerate. Meanwhile, attempts are being made to extract the compound from the root, so that it can be bought in the shops. Another possibility is to mix in garden peat, which contains a parasite that attacks the above named pests.

If you want to be sure that plants are free from parasites, then they should be warmed for 20 minutes in 86°F (30°C) water and then dipped for exactly 10 minutes in 112°F (46°C) water. Afterwards, they should be cooled off immediately in cold water and planted out. Warm water treatment is a somewhat tricky procedure and because of this it is mostly used by large-scale cultivators.

WILD STRAWBERRIES

A pretty border plant, so why not put it in the rockery? This plant has no special soil or care requirements, though sun is necessary, of course! Rügen is a variety without runners, that gives berries from early summer to late autumn. Plant spacing: 10" x 10" (25 cm).

Old plant books say that tea made from wild strawberry leaves is good for diarrhoea and the boiled roots help to get rid of intestinal infections.

RASPBERRIES

100 g raspberries gives:
48 calories
83 g water
1 g protein
0.6 g fat

The raspberry bush came to Britain in the eighteenth century, after it had been cultivated in Greece since the Middle Ages. Now it grows wild — even in the north of Scotland — and is grown fruitfully all over the country. Raspberries are much

9.3 g carbohydrate
41 mg calcium
29 mg phosphorous
12 mg iron
13 units vitamin A
0.07 mg riboflavin
0.3 mg niacin
30 mg vitamin C

more easily cultivated than strawberries and demand much less work.

The raspberry plant is a cane bush that develops shoots (new canes), from buds or "spawn" on the root stem and on the white root branches. In the second year these side canes begin to bear fruit on offshoots.

Most raspberry varieties need support. This can be given in several ways. The easiest method is to bang in 3′ (1 m) high cross pieces at either end of the row, and join each of them to the other with galvanised or plastic coated wire. In this way, you avoid having to tie up each new shoot every year.

In the South, you can plant raspberries in the autumn.

When planting, cut off the shoot just above a bud, to a length of about 12″ (30 cm). It should then be planted shallow or at the same depth as in the nursery. Plant spacing 24″ (60 cm). Row spacing 4′6″ (1½ m).

The canes that have borne fruit should be pruned right down to the ground after the last harvest of the year. You can leave 6−8 of the strongest of the year's canes per each yard. The rest should be cut away. Early the following spring the longest canes can be cut back a little.

After about ten years you should set aside a new raspberry patch, as far away as possible from the previous one.

Varieties

Prussian is the most commonly cultivated variety. It gives large berries and has strong canes that can ultimately do without support or binding. It is not sensitive to raspberry mosaic.

Prussian II is an improved strain with stronger growth.

Asker: has smaller berries, but they taste more like wild raspberries.

Malling Exploit: gives a large yield.

Golden Queen: has yellow berries with a fine, wild raspberry fragrance.

Multiraspa: is a new German strain that is said to be more fruitful than others.

Research is being done to try and breed varieties with the taste of wild pasture raspberries.

Soil conditions

Raspberries grow in most soils in a sunny position, but the best is a loose, leafy moisture retaining soil with a *pH* value of 5−5.6.

Fertilising

Fertilise with manure and compost before planting, then it is enough to fertilize every third year, but any addition of organic material from compost, peat, etc., will increase the yield by helping to retain moisture. After loosening the earth in spring, the soil, around the canes can be covered with hay or dry grass. A raspberry patch should not be limed.

Plant protection

Raspberry beetle:
Raspberry beetle: 4 mm long and light brown. Gnaws holes in the buds and lays its eggs. The larvae are the grubs that are often found in the berries (or not found!). Keep watch for the beetle when the raspberry flowers; shake the canes gently over a bucket and the beetles will eventually drop out.

Raspberry Cane Spot: a fungus disease that discolours the cane, especially around the leaf axils. The plant is weakened and sometimes withers. Thinning is important here. The rows should be airy and light so that the canes dry quickly after the rain. Against small scale attacks, spray with nettle water and cut away the infected canes. If the disease has got a hold, it is best to cut down all canes, hoe the ground and do without one year's harvest, of course.

It is said that raspberry leaf tea is good for bronchial conditions, kidney ailments and rheumatism.

BLACKBERRIES

100 g blackberries gives:
47 calories
85 g water
1.2 g protein
1.1 g fat
7.8 g carbohydrate
17 mg calcium
34 mg phosphorous
0.9 mg iron
30 units vitamin A
0.02 mg thiamine
0.07 mg riboflavin
0.3 mg niacin
5 mg vitamin C

These black or dark red raspberry-like berries first ripen in September. There are several varieties that grow wild, but they are sensitive to very cold conditions.

Plant in the spring, in a warm, sunny sheltered spot, preferably against a wall. Plant spacing: 4½' (1½ m). Some varieties need covering in the winter.

A hardy and thornless variety is the Brom-do-lo.

Bedford Giant can become 15' (5 m) high and is also hardy, but its sharp thorns make picking difficult.

The long canes must be tied up. In autumn they can be loosened and laid on the ground and covered with fir branches, etc. The berries are picked on ripening. They need to be really ripe to taste good and sweet. After picking the canes are cut back in the same way as raspberries.

Soil conditions

Leafy well-drained soil in a warm and sunny place.

Fertilising
See raspberries.

Plant protection
See raspberries.

BOYSENBERRIES

A cross between blackberries and raspberries, with long, rather maleable canes. The berries are big, 1½″ (3 cm) long and dark red.

BLACKCURRANTS

100 g blackcurrants gives:
39 calories
85 g water
1.2 g protein
0.2 g fat
7.7 g carbohydrate
60 mg calcium
43 mg phosphorous
1.3 mg iron
40 units vitamin A
0.03 mg thiamine
0.14 mg riboflavin
0.3 mg niacin
180 mg vitamin C

Blackcurrant bushes can be large, 6′ x 6′ (2 m), and therefore need space. Even in a shady space, they give good yields. As blackcurrants begin growing early in the spring, they should be planted in the autumn, even in northern regions. Plant spacing: 8′ (2½ m). At the planting stage the branches are pruned to a length of about 6″ (15 cm). Plant a little more deeply than is usually instructed. Mulching with hay, etc. under and around the bushes increases the fertility of the soil and prevents weeds.

In the autumn you should thin out the old branches and cut back those that have borne fruit for several years.

Support is sometimes necessary for older bushes with hanging branches. The easiest method is to knock in four piles with cross sections and let the branches rest on these.

In smaller gardens it may be preferable to grow blackcurrants in stem form or on a trellice, to exploit the sun and for better quality.

Blackcurrants can be dried or deep frozen. Even the leaves can be used for tea and in cooking.

Varieties

The choice depends on where your garden is. Ask your nursery.

Wellington XXX has specially high vitamin content but is vulnerable to the big bud disease. It is a middle crop.

Soil requirements

Blackcurrants grow anywhere the soil is not too dry. Hay, etc, around the bushes will help retain the moisture.

Fertilising

Before planting, fertilise the plot with natural fertiliser and repeat every other or every third year. Each spring, compost and add some wood ash if you have it.

Plant protection

Big bud disease is caused by very small (0.2 mm long) insects that live in the blackcurrant buds and cause them to swell up into yellow balls and dry up. There is nothing else to do but immediately dig up and burn infected plants. Use preventive methods for other diseases. At the same time as spraying the fruit trees with skimmed milk during budding, one can dowse the berry bushes as well. Yearly spraying with a silicon preparation generally strengthens the plants' resistance. After about 15 years you should plant new bushes on new ground.

REDCURRANTS

100 g redcurrants gives:
41 calories
83 g water
1.0 g protein
0.2 g fat
8.5 g carbohydrate
36 mg calcium
30 mg phosphorous
1.3 mg iron
12 units vitamin A
0.05 mg thiamine
0.07 mg riboflavin
0.3 mg niacin
30 mg vitamin C

Redcurrant bushes do not become as large as blackcurrant bushes. Plant spacing: 4—5' (1½ m).

Red and white currants develop from two year old shoots and pruning should allow for this. The shoots of newly planted bushes are cut back to 6" lengths and the weaker shoots are cut away altogether.

The first pruning can be treated as thinning the bush of other branches to let light and air in.

Varieties

Jonkheer van Tets is a variety with large, sweet berries.

Red Lake (middle crop) is the most winter-hardy variety. Sweet berries.

Red Dutch (middle crop) can be grown throughout Sweden. Gives a heavy yield, but the berries are very sour.

Red Cross has large, very sweet berries.

White Currants

White currants are sweeter and have a milder taste than red currants. They are good to eat straight from the bush and also favoured for wine making. Knutstorps Sparkling, a Swedish wine of international class, is made from white currants.

GOOSEBERRIES

100 g gooseberries gives:
37 calories
88 g water
0.8 g protein
0.4 g fat
7.2 g carbohydrate
28 mg calcium
34 mg phosphorous
0.3 mg iron
30 units vitamin A
0.15 mg thiamine
0.06 mg riboflavin
0.3 mg niacin
15 mg vitamin C

Gooseberries have the same soil and fertilizer requirements as blackcurrants. Plant spacing: $4'-6'$ (1½—2 m). The bushes can be $5'$ (1½ m) high and as wide. Nowadays there are varieties that are mildew resistant, even though these are not as big and tasty as the more sensitive gooseberries.

The *Hinnonmäki* yellow and reds and the *Resistenta* are all resistant varieties.

Those that are not include *Whitewash*, a middle crop, and green, and *Achilles*, late, large, dark-red, smooth — recommended.

Soil requirements and fertilising

Red and white currants and gooseberries:— the same as blackcurrants.

Plant protection

An old remedy against mildew is to stick freshly cut twigs in and around the gooseberry bushes. Another remedy is to spray with a boiled solution of Tansy. A trick to try with an already infected bush is to make a small bonfire of damp leaves underneath it. The smoke kills the fungus spores.

The gooseberry saw fly's caterpillar can soon eat the leaves of the bushes. You must watch out for them and other grubs and handpick them, or use a hose to spray them away.

WORCESTER BERRIES

These taste and look like a cross between gooseberries and blackcurrants. Their taste is sharper than gooseberries and they are used fresh, for jellies and for wine making. The bush is hardy, undemanding and very productive.

CULTURED BLUEBERRIES (American Giant bilberries)

100 g blueberries gives:
47 calories
84 g water
0.8 g protein
0.3 g fat
10.1 g carbohydrate
20 mg calcium
1 mg phosphorous
1.6 mg iron
10 units vitamin A
0.04 mg thiamine
0.01 mg riboflavin
16 mg niacin
16 mg vitamin C

The bushes grow to 3′ (1 m) high and the berries, which taste nearly as good as ordinary blueberries, are as big as cherries. The bush blooms with white or rose-coloured flowers in May. Plant spacing of 6′ (2 m). *Bluecrop* and the sweet-berried *Goldraube* have shown themselves to be hardy plants.

Bushes should be thinned if they become too thick.

Dried blueberries are a useful remedy for diarrhoea and tea made from dried blueberry leaves is said to stimulate the body's insulin production.

Soil requirements

Light, leafy, sand-mixed soil with a low lime content (*pH* value 4.5—5). Bushes grow best in a shady spot. Covering the ground with peat or hay will help to retain moisture.

Fertilising

Blueberries are not particularly nutrition needy, but composting each year and natural fertilising before planting will benefit the plants.

Storage

First some important rules:

Vegetables must be stored in the dark.

The best temperature is about $36°$ F $(2°$ C).

Most vegetables shrivel if stored too dry. The humidity should be about 85—90%.

Good ventilation.

A reasonably large stone cellar is, of course, the best place for storing your crops.

Potatoes can be stored in large wooden boxes on the floor.

Root vegetables, such as carrots, beetroots, parsnips, swedes and kohlrabi are best preserved in boxes containing wet sand. They are actually biennial plants and are therefore suppose; to remain in the soil one more season.

If they are placed in sand they retain their juiciness and do not shrivel.

Leeks and celery should be harvested as late as possible. After trimming the roots and leaves, place them in boxes filled with earth.

The white cabbage is taken up, with its root and laid, roots uppermost, on well-ventilated shelves.

Green cabbage and brussel sprouts can be left in the ground and harvested when required; make sure you get them before the rabbits do, though!

Onions are best stored by hanging them in bunches in a dry, cool place.

If there is no cellar available, then you can bury a barrel or cement ring in the garden near the house, or build a storage mound as shown in the drawing.

The barrel or cement ring should be covered with a lid and then with hay or evergreen branches.

Deep freezing is a good way to preserve the freshness of vegetables for winter meals. Drying is another method.

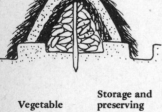

Vegetable	Storage and preserving	Ideal Temp.	Treatment	Storage time
Berries	Deep freeze jam, juice			
Beans.				
runner	deep freeze		boil for 3 mins.	
wax	deep freeze		boil for 3 mins.	
broad	dry		shell	
soya	dry		whole plant hung to dry.	
kidney	dry		shell	

Dill	deep freeze	chop package	
	dry, salt	hang in bunches	
Chicory	stored in earth in cellar		
Fennel	Cellar or deep freeze	boiled	1 month fresh
Cucumber	deep freeze	frozen slices in vinegar	2—3 weeks fresh
Iceburg lettuce	Cellar or fridge +4°C		
Jerusalem artichokes	Stored in earth in cellar		3 weeks
Herbs	dry or deepfreeze	rinse, hang in bunches. Chop up.	
Cabbage, white & red	Cellar 0°C	outside leaves cut away. Root remains	autumn—spring.
Savoy	Cellar	cleansed	4—6 weeks
Celery	Cellar	cleansed	4—6 weeks
Brussel sprouts	In ground or cellar		
Green cabbage	In ground or cellar		
Cauliflower	deep freeze	boiled for 3 mins.	3 weeks fresh
Broccoli	deep freeze	boiled for 3 mins.	5 weeks fresh
Kohlrabi	earth in cellar	roots trimmed	
Onions	cool & dry +1°C	hang in bunches	autumn—spring
Leeks	earth in cellar +1°C	cut off leaves & roots	autumn—spring
Chives	earth in cellar		
Spinach & spinach beet	deep freeze	prepared before freezing	
Nettles	dry or freeze	rinse, hang in bunches or chop up.	
Green pepper	deep freeze or cellar	boil for 3 mins.	3 weeks fresh
Parsley	dry, deep freeze	freeze whole or chopped. Hang in bunches or chop up.	
Potato	cellar +6°C	harvested in dry weather	autumn—spring
Root crops	damp sand in cellar 0°C	harvested in dry weather	autumn—spring
Celeriac	earth in cellar 0°C		autumn—spring
Rhubarb	deep freeze	boil immediately for 5 mins.	
Asparagus	deep freeze	boil for 1 min.	
Tomato	deep freeze	peel, mash up juice:	
Squash & marrow	cellar or cool pantry +8°C		autumn—spring
Peas:			
split	dry	shell	
marrowfat	dry	shell	
sugar	deep freeze	boil for 3 mins:	

Annual weeds

Can be mulched down in hoeing

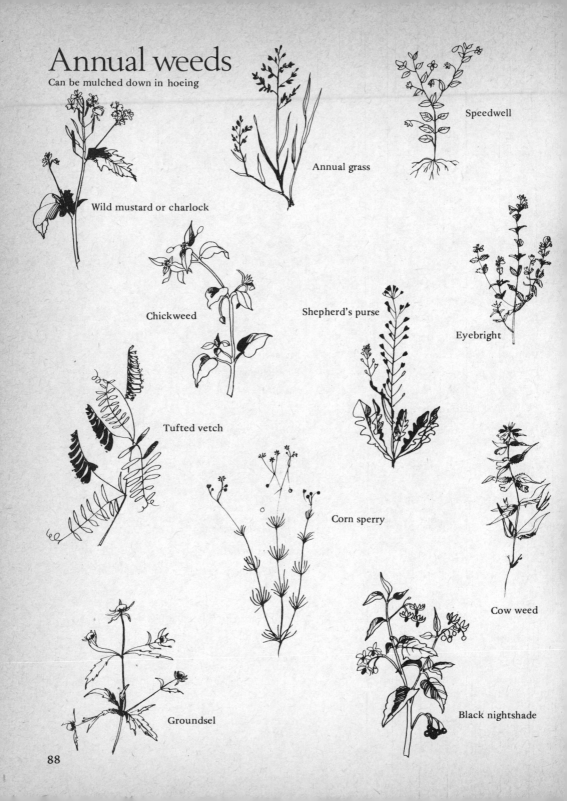

Annual grass

Speedwell

Wild mustard or charlock

Chickweed

Shepherd's purse

Eyebright

Tufted vetch

Corn sperry

Cow weed

Groundsel

Black nightshade

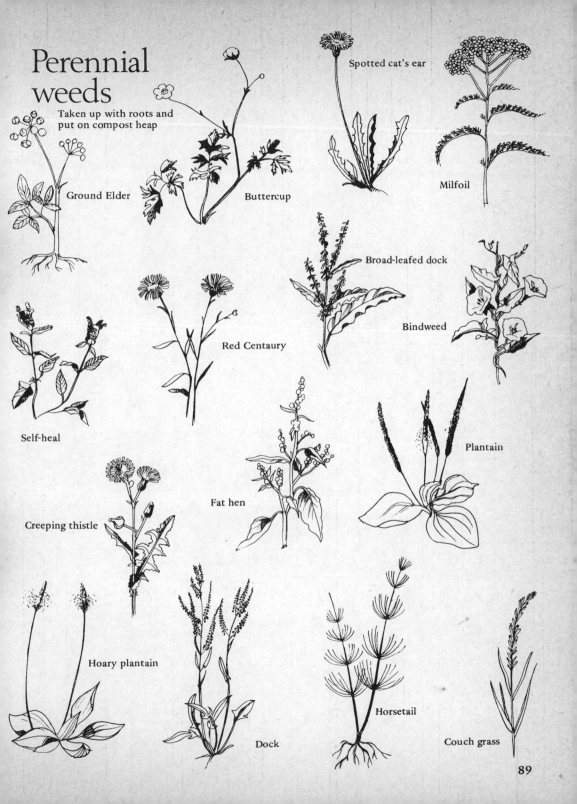

Perennial weeds

Taken up with roots and put on compost heap

Ground Elder

Buttercup

Spotted cat's ear

Milfoil

Self-heal

Red Centaury

Broad-leafed dock

Bindweed

Creeping thistle

Fat hen

Plantain

Hoary plantain

Dock

Horsetail

Couch grass

89

5 years in the garden

Sowings of   19___ 19___ 19___ 19___ 19___ 19___ 19___ 19___ 19___ 19___

_____ ___ ___ ___ ___ ___ ___ ___ ___ ___

_____ ___ ___ ___ ___ ___ ___ ___ ___ ___

_____ ___ ___ ___ ___ ___ ___ ___ ___ ___

_____ ___ ___ ___ ___ ___ ___ ___ ___ ___

_____ ___ ___ ___ ___ ___ ___ ___ ___ ___

_____ ___ ___ ___ ___ ___ ___ ___ ___ ___

_____ ___ ___ ___ ___ ___ ___ ___ ___ ___

_____ ___ ___ ___ ___ ___ ___ ___ ___ ___

_____ ___ ___ ___ ___ ___ ___ ___ ___ ___

_____ ___ ___ ___ ___ ___ ___ ___ ___ ___

_____ ___ ___ ___ ___ ___ ___ ___ ___ ___

_____ ___ ___ ___ ___ ___ ___ ___ ___ ___

_____ ___ ___ ___ ___ ___ ___ ___ ___ ___

_____ ___ ___ ___ ___ ___ ___ ___ ___ ___

_____ ___ ___ ___ ___ ___ ___ ___ ___ ___

_____ ___ ___ ___ ___ ___ ___ ___ ___ ___

_____ ___ ___ ___ ___ ___ ___ ___ ___ ___

_____ 19 __ 19 __ 19 __ 19 __ 19 __ 19 __ 19 __ 19 __ 19 __ 19 __

Planting of   ____ ____ ____ ____ ____ ____ ____ ____ ____ ____

_____ 19 ___ 19 ___ 19 ___ 19 ___ 19 ___ 19 ___ 19 ___ 19 ___ 19 ___ 19 ___

thinning of

	19 __	19 __	19 __	19 __	19 __	19 __	19 __	19 __	19 __	19 __
planted early potatoes										
planted late potatoes										
sown in warm frame										
sown in semi-warm frame										
sown in cold frame										
fertilising										

	19 __	19 __	19 __	19 __	19 __	19 __	19 __	19 __	19 __	19 __
fertilising										
fertilising										
liming										
thinning										
spraying										
spraying										
spraying										
spraying										
compost laid										
compost laid										
compost laid										
first harvest of										
first night of frost										

Soil Analysis

Check your telephone book for the local office of the Ministry of Agriculture, Fisheries & Food. For about £2 they will analyse your soil sample for N (nitrogen), P (phosphorous), for *pH* value and anything else within reason. There are a number of private laboratories who will do the same, but generally charge much more. The Good Gardeners Association, Arkley Manor, Arkley, Herts., carry out soil analysis for Fellows of the Association free of charge (Fellowship £3 p.a.).

Individual general organic information

The Soil Association, Walnut Tree Manor, Haughley, Stowmarket, Suffolk
(tel. 044 970 235)

Information for Market gardens

Organic Farmers and Growers Ltd.,
Longridge, Creeting Road, Stowmarket, Suffolk
(tel. 04492 2845)

Smallholding and companion planting

Henry Doubleday Research Association
20 Convent Lane, Bocking, Braintree, Essex
(tel. 0376 1483)

Biodynamic farming

The Bio-Dynamic Agricultural Association
Sec: John Soper, Broome Farm, Clent, Nr. Stourbridge, Worcs.

Herbs

The Society of Herbalists
Sec: Mrs M. Shanahan, 34 Boscobel Place, London S.W.1

Use of Sprays

Agricultural Development Advisory Service (check your phone book for the local branch)

National Farmers Union
Agriculture House, Knightsbridge, London S.W.1
(tel. 01 235 5077)

Biological Controls

Glasshouse Crops Research Institute
Entymology Section, Rustington, Littlehampton, W. Sussex
(tel. 09064 448128)
Publishes: growers' bulletins on biological controls

Practical Self-Sufficiency   The Ecologist   Seed
popular magazines

Work Weekends On Organic Farms (WWOOF)
For those seeking assistance in terms of practical help, or for those who wish to spend weekends working on organic farms, write to: Rowan Malcolm, 143 Sabine Road London S.W.11

Friends of the Earth
9 Poland Street, London W1
(tel. 01 437 6121)

Overseas
Organic Farming and Gardening Society (Australia)
Sec: John Grierson, Box 265 w, Melbourne 3001, Victoria, Australia
Publishes: *The Good Earth* (quarterly)

Soil Association of South Australia
Pres: Frank A. Langley, 9 Cotham Avenue, Kensington Park 5068, South Australia

Organic Gardening and Farming Society of Tasmania
Hon sec: David Stephen, 12 Delta Avenue, Taroona, Tasmania 7006
Publishes: regular newsletters

Soil Association of New Zealand
Nat sec: R. E. Betteridge, 27 Collins Street, Addington, Christchurch 2, New Zealand
Publishes: *Soil and Health* (bimonthly)

Organic Soil Association of South Africa
Box 47100, P.O. Parklands, Johannesburg, South Africa
Publishes: *Soil Sense* (quarterly)